ESCAPE FROM ASCOLI

Story of evasion and escape

Ken de Souza

Newton Publishers

First published in Great Britain by
Newton Publishers (1989)
Hartfield Road, Cowden, Kent TN8 7JW

ISBN 1-872308-02-3

Every effort has been made by the author and the
publishers to trace owners of copyright material.

Printed and bound by Unwin Brothers Ltd.,
The Gresham Press, Old Woking, Surrey GU22 9LH
A Member of the Martins Printing Group

CONTENTS

Pages

Chapters

1	Caterpillars in the Blue	1
2	Led by a star	9
3	Feet and bones	15
4	Stones and bullets	21
5	The wrong lot	27
6	A question of nationality	37
7	Red double-cross	43
8	Tobruk again!	53
9	Flies undone!	57
10	Hell-ship	61
11	Via Dolorosa	69
12	Hoppers in the straw	75
13	Cattle in transit	81
14	P.G. 70 at Monte Urano	87
15	Red Cross to the rescue	97
16	'The Seventy Times'	101
17	Dixies — with lids	109
18	Below the bridge	115
19	Contadini	119
20	Walk before breakfast	127
21	The priest and the nun	133
22	Contadino — with bike	139
23	Buon' Natale	149
24	Naked to Freedom	157
25	Home	161
	About the Author	163
	RAF Escaping Society	165
	Illustrations between pages	96–97

To Lillian
and to all wives who have ever
known the anguish of waiting

ALAM HALFA — THE FIRST LAND VICTORY

Flying a brand-new Wellington IC bomber, our crew arrived in Egypt on 23rd June, 1942. We were just in time to participate in the Battle of Alam Halfa, the first-ever victory over the German army. Like the first-ever victory over the Luftwaffe in the Battle of Britain this was a defensive victory whereby the aggressors were, by well-directed counter-attacks, thrown into confusion and routed. While we were touching-down at Cairo, the German commander, Erwin Rommel, was advancing towards the 28-mile strip of land between El Alamein on the coast and the impassable Qattara Depression to the south.

We joined 148 squadron a week later, at about the time that Field Marshall Sir Claude Auchinleck, ("The Auk"), was saying: "These damn British have been taught for too long to be good losers. I've never been a good loser. I'm going to win." He strengthened the defensive position in the El Alamein area in such a way as to control the direction of enemy attacks. Although his army had been depleted by supplying reinforcements to other theatres of war, he knew that morale was sky-high. Fighting in the battle-fields of North Africa, every serviceman was fighting none-the-less to prevent the invasion and annihilation of his own country — a probability if the axis forces had gained mastery of the Mediterranean. Italian morale, by contrast, was questionable: many of the rank-and-file had reluctantly left their shops and farmsteads to fight for a cause in which they had no interest or belief. They had been only too ready to surrender early in 1941 to the army of Sir Archibald Wavell.

So it came about even before the battle was joined at Alam Halfa, with his armoured divisions severely reduced in strength, "The Auk" depended very much on the R.A.F. to harass the enemy lines of communication. In July nearly 15,400 sorties were flown.

Thus during our first week on the Squadron we were bombing enemy motorised units south of El Daba and we returned to the attack on 24th and 26th July when Rommel's tanks were some fifty miles closer to our Base. A feature of these operations was the co-operation of the Navy Albacores, dropping flares with marvellous accuracy to illuminate our targets. Apart from this, the task of 148 Squadron Wellingtons was the regular nightly bombing of Tobruk Harbour, the only harbour in the area where Rommel's supplies could be landed.

The battle of Alam Halfa began auspiciously. Field Marshall Auchinleck had ordered the 8th Army armour to stand firm and allow the enemy to come against the British guns. The order was carried out and the Axis forces suffered heavy losses. Then the mobile units, frequently changing the point and direction of their thrusts, struck at the various Italian sectors. These tactics were continued during the remainder of the month and on the second August Rommel wrote: "Our attack came to a halt and our strength failed ... Our chance was irretrievably gone."

As a result of the continued bombing of Tobruk's shipping, harbour installations and supply depots, the enemy remained thin on the ground. Only this can explain the incredible fact that, after baling out south-west of Mersa Matruh, I was able to walk 100 miles straight through supposedly Axis-occupied positions.

On 15th August Field Marshall Montgomery took over command and at Sir Winston Churchill's instigation there began a massive build-up of men and materials. "The Auk" had laid the foundation upon which Monty was to build the ultimate resounding victory of El Alamein.

FOREWORD

During the Second World War many airmen had the misfortune to crash or come down by parachute in enemy territory. To come down in North West Europe was one thing but to come down in the North African desert was quite another matter.

This is the story of an RAF navigator on a night bombing mission to Tobruk in the autumn of 1942 who, together with other members of his crew, was forced to abandon his Wellington bomber by parachute after an engine fire. Landing without injury in the darkness he was unable to make contact with his colleagues who were widely scattered. Alone in the emptiness of the desert without water or food he set off to walk to the Allied lines at Alamein over 100 miles away.

By sheer guts, determination and will power, and by Divine Providence he managed to keep going, surviving the heat of the desert and unbearable thirst, eventually to fall into the hands of the Italian army, this undoubtedly saved his life.

As a prisoner-of-war he was taken to Benghazi with Hal his pilot, and with other Allied prisoners they were shipped in appalling conditions to a prisoner-of-war camp in Italy.

In the autumn of 1943 with the surrender of the Italians, the German army took over control of the prison camp and started preparations for the move of the prisoners to Germany. It was at this time that he and his colleagues had the luck to find a hiding place, and after the departure of the main body of prisoners and the German guards, they were able to make their escape being befriended by a kindly peasant family. After making contact with British forces working behind the lines, they were able to make their way to a rendezvous on the coast to be picked up by a naval torpedo boat.

Ken de Souza has written a fascinating and fast-moving account of his desert survival, his existance in a POW camp and his time amongst the wonderful peasant folk of the Ascoli Province, who took in two total strangers as if they were members of their own family knowing full well the great risks they were taking in sheltering British prisoners. His whole story is vividly described and this book provides a valuable addition to the literaturte of escape and evasion during the Second World War. Underlying it all, and particularly his survival in the desert, is his strong Christian faith and his steadfast belief in the guiding hand of the Almighty leading him to his successful escape and to freedom.

At the end of the war the RAF Escaping Society was formed with the object of contacting the many brave people in all the occupied countries of Europe who had sheltered and given help to our airman at great risk to themselves. During the past 45 years we have kept in touch with these people — our "Helpers" — and we continue to look after those in special need. Today we still have over 2000 names of "Helpers" on our books.

Air Chief Marshall Sir M. Lewis Hodges
KCB, CBE, DSO, DFC.
President RAF Escaping Society.

PREFACE

We were never heroes, Hal and I, just two men separated from their loved ones by the war. In wartime, friends — and enemies — come and go: no one questions their disappearance from the scene. Of all the hundreds who came and went in our lives I've only mentioned those who had some kind of influence on our escape.

Thanks to a freak of R.A.F. posting we too found ourselves together for most of our Service days. By the time we became POW's we had developed that mutual trust which made our escape possible; and we know that our qualities, being completely different, were exactly complementary, making us the ideal escape team.

What we did have in common was our determination to get to our wives. Our plans to achieve this began at the moment of our capture.

THE OP

AIRCRAFT "B" HF840 WELLINGTON IC

148 Squadron — Night 19/20 September, 1942.
Target: Shipping in Tobruk Harbour

Crew:

Captain	— 1260232 Sgt. Curtois. H.L.
2nd Pilot	— 655148 Sgt. Prosser. T.B.
Observer	— 926093 Sgt. de Souza. A.K.
1st Wireless	— 1068103 Sgt. Coles. A.T.
Operator	
Front Gunner	— 1282960 Sgt. Frampton. A.E.
Rear Gunner	Aus. 404572 Sgt. Bullock J.H.T.

Formation flight of WELLINGTON 1c's, transferred from 37 Squadron ME to 148 Squadron ME

In 1939, the Vickers-Armstrong's Wellington was the best machine available to Bomber Command. Much loved by those who flew her, the "Wimpey" was extremely rugged and able to keep flying despite extensive damage. This twin-engined medium bomber was the only bomber type to be produced throughout the War and more aircrew flew in this aircraft than any other because the Wellington formed the back-bone of the Operational Training Units.

ACKNOWLEDGEMENTS

R.A.F. Museum, Hendon
R.A.F. Historical Department — for documents, maps
Ministry of Defence W.D. — and illustrations
Bournemouth Public Libraries
Francesco and Marcella Brugnoni of Sant' Elpidio
Signorina Marzia Malaigia of Monte Urano
The late Signor Zambelli (R.A.F. Escaping Society Italian representative)
Alan Cooper — for much helpful advice
Chaz Bowyer — for illustration of Wellington Ic's
Anne Woodford
Margaret Malyan — for typing and
John Parker — word processing
Lynn Parker
and our son Ian for fetching and carrying.
Illustrations by Derrick Smith

Ken de Souza.

IRVIN GREAT BRITAIN LTD.

CATERPILLAR CLUB

In 1919 at Mc Cook Airfield, U.S.A., Leslie Leroy Irvin demonstrated for the first time that it was possible to fall freely through the air without losing consciousness, open a parachute manually and survive.

Following the successful emergency descents of two United States Air Corps pilots in 1922, Leslie Irvin and other individuals associated with the early parachute business agreed to sponsor the "CATERPILLAR CLUB" and that membership would be open to anyone who had saved their life in an emergency using an Irvin-type safety parachute. The European branch of the Club was formed in 1926.

Today, sixty-three years later, more than forty nationalities are represented in the European Club membership of just under 32,000 and worldwide it is estimated that the total number of lives saved has exceeded 100,000. As would be expected, the largest number of applications was made between 1939 and 1945 — many from prisoner-of-war camps.

The only rule governing acceptance into the CATERPILLAR CLUB is that applicants shall have saved their life in a genuine emergency descent by an Irvin-type parachute in circumstances where they had no intention of jumping at the commencement of the flight!!

The privileges of membership are a distinct pin in the shape of a Caterpillar, a membership card and — last but not least — THE CONTINUED ENJOYMENT OF LIFE.

Eileen Robinson
October 1989

PROLOGUE

The Cowshed

Fiftythree pairs of critical eyes were focussed on the new teacher perched on the high chair at the high desk. They watched him as he dipped the school steel-nibbed pen into the school red-ink well and begin:

"John Adams?"

"Sir!" from a bright-eyed scrap of a lad at the heating-pipe end of the back row.

"Peter Allen?"

"Here Sir!" 'Here" was the narrow space between desk-ledge and seat into which tubby Peter had managed to squeeze himself.

Teacher, sallow and aquiline, carefully made the statutory red oblique in the register, a precise diagonal from bottom to top of the printed rectangle. In these early post-war days inspectors still judged a teacher by the way he or she kept the Register. He hesitated, remembering what the Head had told him:

"Peter lives with his grandparents. His Mum and Dad were both killed in the London blitz. Peter was brought out of the rubble unharmed."

The children down there in front of him began whispering but stopped abruptly as he continued:

"William Appleton?"

"Yes Mr de Zusie." Tall tousled-haired William was another war casualty. Dad, an air-gunner, had "bought it" over Kiel. His plane had received a direct hit. William had been five years old at the time.

He went on alphabetically down the Register, down through the list of boys then down through the list of girls. Born in 1939 or 1940, they were all war casualties, some more than others. The Head could only tell him about a few of the cases. He reached the last name:

"Anne Yeats?"

"Yes Mr Doozy!" was the whispered reply. Her classmates tittered and poor Anne rounded her eyes and put her hand over her mouth because she knew she'd got it wrong.

"That's alright, Anne," he assured her, "It's not an easy name to learn. Anyway you'll see it on the classroom door."

Anne didn't know then that she had coined the nickname which was to remain with him for 35 years.

As he got down from the chair the open Register began to slide down the sloping desk.

xiii

A small boy scuttled forth to pick up the pink blotting-paper before Sir put his foot thereon.

"Thanks laddie," as he carefully blotted the red ink. Then taking up his second school steel-nibbed pen he dipped it into the school blue-ink well and wrote the total at the bottom of the column. At the start of the afternoon session he'd make red obliques from top to bottom, thus completing a column of upside-down vees. At the end of the week an exquisite red herring-bone pattern would be revealed. Unless somebody spoilt it by being absent in which case a circle with the school blue-ink pen would mark the spot. When illness struck, the herring-bone was interspersed with rows of identical blue noughts.

He raised the desk-lid and placed the Holy Book safely inside. Then unable to postpone the moment any longer, he turned and faced the class, fifty-three children of all shapes and sizes, fitted into desks which had already served at least a couple of generations. Tubby Peter wasn't the only misfit. At least his feet reached the floor-boards. Lofty Williams plimsolled feet also rested on the floor but he sat hunched with his knees nearly up to his chin. Only John Adams, the first boy on the Register exactly fitted his desk. Most of the other hundred feet dangled, some still, some swinging; and of the swinging brigade some slyly kicking their neighbours.

He found himself thinking of the Italian children of six years ago. Pierrino would be eighteen now, a seller of fruit like his papa, but at that time he was a mischievous-looking lad much like John Adams here, taller of course but with the same sparkle in his eyes. And Vincensina had been shy like Anne, her hands also fluttering to her face every time she made a mistake, Caterina, Giuseppina, little Tomasso and large-limbed Umberto — they all had their parallels here. Yet he had been so much closer to the bambini because the class had never numbered more than a dozen. To get to know, really know and understand, each one of these fifty-three that was a daunting task indeed! Yet if he were to succeed with them it had somehow to be achieved.

"John Adams and Peter Allen, will you please give out the exercise books?"

He couldn't have chosen more unwisely. To get to the front of the class John had to crawl under a couple of desks, slide in between another couple, collide with Peter who was still trying to get out of his seat and make a final sprint down the narrow aisle at the front.

"These books, Sir?" he panted, picking up one of the blue writing books from one of the ledges at the side of the high desk.

Doozy gave a second packet to Peter when at last he arrived, red-faced and embarrassed.

"Count them into piles of eight, please Peter. John take one pile at a time to the end of each row." Then addressing the class, "Supposing we had 56 children in the room, how many piles of 8 would we need?"

Various guesses were forthcoming before he noticed fair-haired Tom Locksley at the middle of the front row, his arm patiently raised.

"Seven Mr de Souza. Actually there are five people in our row, not eight, so there'll be three books over."

He became aware of Tom's neighbour, smiling David Streeter, his arm raised.

"Yes David?"

The children were amazed that on this, the first day of term, the new teacher called them all by their names. In fact the previous night he had learnt the seating plan by heart.

David stood up to make the polite observation that as there were only 24 exercise books in a packet, John and Peter would be five books short . . .

When he had taught another half-dozen classes Doozy was to hear that both Tom and David had been admitted to University . . .

Prior to calling the Register he had distributed shining new pencils and now, before they'd had time to be chewed, blunted or broken, he got the children to make proper use of them by filling in the book labels according to the example he had set out on the blackboard.

With John and Peter safely back in their places, he himself gave out the other sets of books, taking out a packet at a time from the tall cupboard partly hidden by the blackboard and easel.

As there was only the one cupboard Doozy had brought in a couple of orange-boxes to contain the children's reading-books. Standing endwise they made useful book-shelves and, with the flowered curtains Lillian had made, looked really attractive, a welcome touch of colour in that drab classroom.

For that matter all the classrooms were drab, the whole building was drab and dented and, in places, rusty. Yet on entering it for the first time he had sensed the spirit of the place, an atmosphere of caring and compassion that had always belonged here.

He had felt this even before he had met the old couple who lived on the corner of Martin Road. It wasn't really a road, just a rough track leading into the broom and gorse and heather that covered the hillside. The building had been erected on a stony plateau halfway up the hill. In a brief chat they had told him the history of its foundation . . .

It was a week before the beginning of term, the day he'd brought the second of the orange-boxes, the bike-basket heavy with books. He'd leaned his sit-up-and-beg against the garden fence because the orange-box was slipping off the handlebars.

"Reckon you're the new teacher, Sir. Pleased to meet you!"

The voice had come from the row of runner beans and the grizzled old man in a check shirt had emerged to steady the box while he re-tied it. "Bill," he called himself.

"Wonder you didn't break your bloomin' neck carrying that lot over the Alps!" . . .

He recalled Bill's words, threading his way between the desks and watching the children write their labels . . .

"The Alps" were the three steep hills separating Martin Road from the Bournemouth boundary.

"I walk most of the way up the hills," he said apologetically. Bill had just grinned then looked across at the long green corrugated-iron building.

" 'Tis a good old school, bin goin' since 1920 and they've had some good teachers there — no nonsense, you know. You couldn't find a happier bunch o' kids nowhere. I mind the time when trucks brought in all them sheets o' corrugated and dumped them here on our common. Just a year after the Armistice that was — I hadn't been demobbed no more 'n a few months."

"Twas a recreation hut for the Army hospital up Salisbury Plain," had chimed in Bill's wife, limping across to the fence, a bowlful of runners under her arm. "The Education bought it for two thousand pounds, they say." The she'd turned to her husband and chuckled, "Go on Bill. Tell 'un what they calls the place!"

Slowly, deliberately Bill had wiped his eyes with the corner of a large handkerchief before replying:

"Nothin' to do with the school, you know — just the building. The cow-shed! Tis what everybody calls it." . . .

He stood at the back of the classroom now looking down on the heads of the children, bowed over their work; then above the heads at the partitions between this and the two adjoining rooms — higher than those between cattle-stalls but partitions none-the-less. Above the partitions were the rafters where the school cat prowled.

He supposed he was the only member of staff who had actually taught in a real cattle-shed. His mind went back to those two bitter cold January days in Ascoli when for some reason the farmhouse kitchen wasn't available for lessons. He'd taken the bambini down there because it was a warm place, the warmth emanating from the bodies of the champing oxen. Hal, sitting close to the small dusty window had tried to concentrate on his book while they'd sung English nursery rhymes, worked at mental arithmetic and played guessing games. As lessons proceeded he'd forgotten the smell of the oxen, something which the contadini children seemed never to notice at all . . .

The handbell being rung in the corridor signalled the time of milk-drinking. The books were packed into neat piles and he supervised the movement of children to the front of the class.

"Mr de Zusie, Sir," asked William Appleton between sucks at his straw, "Was you in the RAF?" When Doozy nodded, the boy said proudly, "So was my Dad, Sir" . . .

The empty third-of-a-pint bottles clattered back into the crates as the children filed out for morning break. He remained at one of the four large windows looking out at the broom and lupins and roses in the school garden.

Beyond the garden up near the top of the slope the air was full of swallows and martins. Later that day, as he was wheeling his bike out of the gate, a flight of swifts screamed low over his head and then put on a dazzling display of low-flying aerobatics.

Summer faded into Autumn and just as imperceptibly Doozy and the children got to understand each other.

They'd thought him odd when on the second day he'd leapt on to one of the front desks and rotated the gas-bracket arm to the North-South line. The Head had watched horrified through the corridor window as he'd hung the label NORTH at one end, then jumped down to draw star constellations on the blackboard. Why did Doozy think North so important? Surely it mattered more to know the number of one's bus and the names of the roads near one's home.

Or, like John Adams, you might be writing a surreptitious note to pass along the heating-pipe to your pal in the class next door — a simple operation in times past. Now, when you turned to show your classmate, you found, not your classmate but Doozy sitting next to you. If you drew funny pictures in your Arithmetic book, there he was peering over your shoulder. He had a trick of moving around the the room without any sound at all — except when he tore his trousers on the iron-framed desks. Then he'd fetch a hammer to blunt the sharp bits of metal.

For History Doozy had pinned large sheets of paper to cover the whole length of the top half of the classroom wall. He couldn't safely stick drawing-pins in the lower half because the hardboard was thin and the pin-points protruded on the other side. The children would be cutting letters and figures from coloured gummed paper while he'd be standing on an old newspaper on a desk.

On this particular day, around Michaelmas it was, he was up there calling for the letters he needed for the Chart.

"Has somebody made us a C?"

"Me Sir." Angel-haired Alan Billington reached up and Doozy reached down. When he had stuck on the C he asked for the R, then the O, then the M and so on, each child bringing forward a letter until the final L was put up.

"Cromwell's the road up the hill, Mr de Zusie," informed William.

"The road is named after a man who lived about three hundred years ago," replied Doozy from on high, "He was a dictator, the only dictator our country ever had."

"Was he bad like Itterler?" asked Mary Huxter, shaking her long flaxen plaits. Mary's Mum had been a WAAF stationed up at Ibsley aerodrome.

"No Mary, not like Hitler, but he signed to have the King's head chopped off and that was a bad thing." Now Allan Billington's hand was raised, his pale blue eyes looked up imploringly.

"P-please Sir, will you tell us how you escaped from a prison-camp?"

Miss Hatchard in the next-door classroom had told her class about it and ever since then these children had been pestering him for the story. He knew that, as a result of being a prisoner-of-war, Alan's Dad was now a chronic invalid.

Yet what should he tell these young children about the war and would history books ever tell the truth? Would future generations understand that the British people "in their finest hour" had by their supreme courage escaped not only invasion, but complete annihilation? But it had been a close call ...

"P-please Sir, won't you tell us!" The blue eyes never wavered.

Doozy looked down at the sea of upturned eager faces, great kids, the salt of the earth, the stuff of which real history is made. There were other faces among them, too: Caterina and Pierrino, Vincensina and Umberto, Giuseppinna and Tomasso — all grand little people.

"One day, Alan," promised Doozy ...

CHAPTER 1

Caterpillars in the blue

"For Gawd's sake, Ken, drop those bloody bombs!" That was Cockney Alf in the Wellington front turret. He had the best view of the flak which was bursting ever closer.

The toy ship in Tobruk harbour moved along the bomb-sight drift-wires agonisingly slowly. So slowly that, for a fleeting moment of panic, I wondered if I'd fitted the correct height bar. I checked. Yes, it was the 500-pound bar sure enough.

"Right!" I told Hal, insurance manager turned pilot for the war.

A blast of flak from "Erik" shook the old Wimpy and Hal over-corrected.

"Left — left!" I rebuked him.

The toy lined itself up perfectly.

"Steady — steady!" pressing the tit with the setting on "salvo". "Bombs gone!"

As the bomb-doors closed, the fingers of light that had been rummaging around the sky, finally clutched and coned us, lighting us up with terrifying brilliance.

Hal pushed the stick right forward and we screamed down towards the water leaving the searchlight to grope as best it might. Momentarily the harbour was lost from my view as I glimpsed the murky blackness of the Med. My stomach seemed to have stayed up at 6000 feet. The rest of me was about to perish in the Big Splash. Or maybe we'd be destroyed by the blast from our own exploding bombs.

The blazing oil installations lit up the strained faces of Hal and second-pilot Bryn. They were both heaving back mightily on the stick. Faced with the nigh impossible, Wellington T2878 shuddered violently. In those days bombers were not supposed to come out of vertical dives.

For one gasping moment she staggered, her whole frame shaking. Any other aircraft would certainly have fallen apart. But somehow or other she took control of herself.

Painfully she reared up, narrowly missing a jib-crane. Then gathering momentum, up through the inferno of flak she climbed, up and up towards the stars. Her Pegasus engines rasped triumphantly.

Once again the Wimpy's geodetic construction had saved us. It was garden trellis, wrought in duralumin and moulded in the shape of an aeroplane. The stresses were distributed with uncanny precision. It was this construction which had saved our lives when a tyre had burst on take-off back in England.

1

ESCAPE FROM ASCOLI

That Wimpy had ripped her belly out but we had escaped unharmed. Likewise over the Western Desert a large section of fabric had peeled off the mainplane. But the near-skeleton had returned safely to Base.

"O.K. Bryn, I've got her," said Hal, his touch on the controls now feather-light.

"Steer 150 degrees," I counselled, "We'll get to Hell out of here and then I'll give you a course for Base."

"Reckon you overshot that boat, Ken. Seems you've got a cosy fire going on the quay, though," drawled Bert, our Aussie in the rear turret.

"Must have been one of the other kites!" jibed Taffy the Wireless, "Ken usually puts 'em in the spaces!"

"Shut up, can't you!" snapped Hal, "Intercomm. silence, or we'll be picked up by fighters!"

The turmoil of Tobruk faded. No sound now but the purring Peggies.

I rescued my Sextant and Course-and-Speed Calculator which were strewn around the floor. Lucky I'd tied on my pencils — a necessary precaution against our thieving crew!

From the astrodome with the hand-compass I took a back-bearing on the burning quayside. Normally I'd have asked Bert to do that by sighting his guns on it and reading the angle shown on the calibrated turret azimuth. But Hal had rightly commanded intercomm. silence.

"Estimated position 20 m. SW TOBRUK. New course 100°C." I wrote the message-slip and took it up to Hal. Back then to the nav. table to plot it on the Mercator's chart; thence again to the astrodome to take a running-fix.

The Pegasus engines went on purring as if nothing had happened and three-and-a-half uneventful hours later we descended through the early-morning sand-haze to land safely at Base.

Our C.O., Wing-Commander Warne, raced up in his jeep to greet us at dispersal.

"All O.K., boys?"

Hal gave the thumbs-up sign and nodded: "Bit of trouble with the searchlights Sir. Otherwise fine!"

Wing-Co. grinned and roared off to check the next returning aircraft.

In the underground de-briefing room we only mentioned the power-dive because the aircraft structure needed extra-careful checking before T2878 was taken up again. Apart from that it had no operational significance.

In the Sergeants' Mess understatement was the key-word, near-disasters were jocularly referred to as "shaky-do's" and those who had paid the ultimate price were said to have — "bought it". Life was for Today; it was bad form to dwell upon yesterday or talk of tomorrow. Privately one prayed.

Like everybody else I'd had my share of shaky-do's and, having survived them in the past, I'd convinced myself that I was likely to do so in the future. Fallacious reasoning where the wish was father to the thought!

Even my very first flight was a shaky-do. Hard to believe it was only

2

eighteen months ago three of us sprog-observers went up for "air experience" with poor Sergeant Dindorf. Like all Polish pilots he was desperate to attack the thugs who had murdered his country. Training Command flying was sheer frustration which he expressed by diving at the Porthcawl cliffs and pulling out in the nick of time. I was lying in the open bomb hatch of the Fairey Battle, absolutely terrified. It was equally terrifying for the trainee in the open gun-turret and perhaps even more so for our in-between companion who could only catch fleeting glimpses of earth, sky and eternity.

They were incredibly brave pilots, those Poles whose fighter squadron performed so valiantly in the Battle of Britain.

A fortnight later I went up again with Sergeant Dindorf to practise bomb-aiming.

And only the following week of April, 1941, alone in the Battle, he bought it by hitting the cliff.

But the shakiest of shaky-do's was crashing in a Blackburn Botha two months later. Throughout their short but bloody history Bothas had had a nasty habit of maiming or killing those who flew in them.

Sergeant Ardley throttled back as we made our approach to Bobbington Airfield and down below on the golf-course a woman in a car was watching us. She must have been as horrified as we were when the starboard engine suddenly retched and stopped. As the Botha dived towards her, she hurriedly started her car and moved, as she thought, to a place of safety.

Although we knew that nose-diving into the ground was normally fatal, we hopefully took up crash positions, Sergeant sliding open the roof.

I lay on the floor bracing myself against the bulkhead.

Ironic that my last moments of life should be the day after my love's birthday.

The uprushing ground gathered speed.

Absurd that it should all end here before I'd even had a chance to strike one blow to protect my love, my family, my country against the thugs.

The sky disappeared from the open roof. I had a close-up of gorse-flowers and heather and green sward as the fearful crash went on and on and on — not just one final impact exploding into eternity as I'd expected.

An agonising rending of metal, perspex, wood and glass. A tearing-asunder of wires. A strange numbness in my being which at first I mistook for death.

Then, smelling petrol, I struggled to my feet, climbed over the bulkhead and somehow scrambled through the open roof. As the Botha was canted over on her side it was only a short drop to the ground. However, when I landed, my right leg buckled under me. As fast as I was able, I crawled away, desperate to be at a safe distance when the plane burst into flames.

But it didn't happen — only a slow-rising dust-cloud and an uncanny silence. No voice, no sound nor any sign of life . . .

Then, suddenly appearing, a man on a bike.

"Are you all right?" he asked, incredulously, and then, as I tried to get up, "No — no! Don't move, laddie. Let me have a look at you."

A First-Aider he was who found a stick to splint my nearly-severed right leg, who immobilised my fractured right arm, who cleansed the worst of my wounds before the ambulance came.

The hospital doctor held out little hope, but my love cycled twenty miles to Cosford that hot June day. Twenty miles there and twenty miles back through the 1941 heatwave, thunderstorms included!

Because I always knew she would be coming back next day, I hung on. And because of the brilliance of the Polish surgeon who treated me, I recovered completely, passed the stringent aircrew medical and flew again exactly three months later, my pilot Sergeant Ardley.

The impact had thrown him out through the open roof-hatch and he'd landed relatively unharmed in a bush. The second trainee-navigator had had a similar escape. However the Botha had demolished the car, killing the lady-driver. If only she'd stayed where she was! . . .

And sadly the wireless operator had bought it: the starboard engine had been torn off in the crash, penetrating the radio position.

Ardley gave me the thumbs-up sign before starting the take-off run. Sweetly the Avro Anson took to the air. The Bothas — thank God! — had been taken out of service.

After that shaky-do I could take all in my stride, such as flak over Tobruk. Strange that when the explosions were deafening and the Wimpy was jolted around the sky, we got back to Base absolutely intact — not a hole anywhere in the fuselage. Yet on what we considered quiet nights we would end up like a colander!

Next operation after the searchlight affair, an exploding shell cracked the triplex bomb-aiming window under me — a near shaky-do.

Then soon after midnight on 19th/20th September, while cruising over the tranquil Bay of Sollum, we were astounded to see a tongue of flame poke out of our port engine. It popped in again and, a second later, poked out once more, longer and redder and accompanied by very rude noises. The Wimpy bucked like a shying nag.

"Port engine on fire," commented Hal laconically. Then leaning forward and operating the necessary control, he added, "Automatic extinguisher on."

The tongue flickered, blanched and presently disappeared. The Pegasus engine now sounded like a heavily-armoured knight clattering down from his horse. We slewed round towards the little town of Bardia and began to lose height. The propeller blades became visible, idling in the rushing air.

"No panic, she'll fly on one engine," said Hal confidently, levelling her out at 5000 feet and making a 180-degree turn.

I jettisoned the bombs. The recipients down there must have been very surprised. By the time I'd sat down again at the Navigator's table, Bardia was drifting away behind us as our starboard engine took up the challenge. Soon the bay itself disappeared from view.

4

CHAPTER 1   CATERPILLARS IN THE BLUE

With the sextant I tried a shot of Polaris. It was as I'd expected. The sextant bubble clung obstinately to the circumference of the illuminated circle of vision. We were flying straight all right, but certainly not level. We were gradually losing height. Hal and Pete would know this from the behaviour of the altimeter needle. As for Bert and Alf and Taffy, now breathing sighs of relief, no need to alarm them for the present.

Their relief manifested itself in a burst of conversation. This time Hal didn't check them.

"Cairo here I come!" exulted Bert Bullock.

"I knew it! Bert's off to see that luscious bint in Groppi's!" That was Taffy Coles.

"Too right I am!" retorted Bert, "Gotta date this afternoon."

"Cor!" from the front turret and a ribald Cockney chuckle, "She'll make your tail wag!"

"We don't call him 'tail-end Charlie' for nothing!" put in Hal, anxious to keep up morale.

"Compass Course for Base 135 degrees," I told Hal, handing him a message-slip for confirmation.

I plotted it on my Mercator's, setting off the wind velocity at 5000 feet, a mere 10 m.p.h. from 045 degrees. The resulting track should keep us clear of fighter interception. Later we could alter course directly for our destination. But there was the rub — what destination? I doubted whether we'd have enough fuel to limp back to Base — 40 kilometres south of Cairo.

Our range depended on our flying at the optimum economic air speed at the optimum economic height 130 m.p.h. at 8000 feet. We would all-too-soon be at half that height and, in order to keep above stalling speed, Hal had pushed the revs well up. The dead engine must also have acted like a brake. Overcoming this retarding factor would also increase consumption.

I decided that the critical moment would come at a point midway between south of Buqbuq and south of Sidi Barrani. If we didn't alter course then, we could run out of fuel deep in the desert; if we altered course earlier we could find ourselves mixing it with the Ju. 88s.

We were making a Ground Speed of 96 m.p.h., and with my dividers I stepped this off along the track-line to mark in the position where I intended to alter course.

Returning to the astrodome, I sensed immediately that something was wrong. Like the time when, after an unusually hectic visit to Tobruk, Hal had flown red-on-black, and we'd made a reciprocal course in the direction of Erik's gunsights.

It wasn't a reciprocal now, but, little by little, we were edging to starboard.

Even as the thought crossed my mind, the starboard Peggy uttered a short metallic cough. The intercomm. was suddenly silent, everyone of us listening, praying maybe. Presently Hal muttered, "Revs are dropping," and we were shaken by a cough more violent than the first. We began to lose height more rapidly.

5

ESCAPE FROM ASCOLI

The Wimpy's whole frame set up a feverish shuddering sending my protractor, dividers and parallel-rulers chasing each other across the chart. My desk navigator's-lamp trembled in its bracket!

"Throw everything you can overboard!" ordered Hal.

I started with the 4-pound incendiaries and the flares, pushing them one after another down the flare-chute. A resulting string of fires marked our track over the ground. Bert and Alf would be jettisoning their Brownings with the belts of ammo. and handfuls of discarded links. In spite of this our angle of descent remained dangerously steep, and at every splutter of the engine we dropped another fifty feet or so.

Hal and Bryn were making a last effort to level her out, but it was hopeless. The starboard Peggy was misfiring badly and we were already down to 1200 feet. The minimum bale-out height for the aircrew-type parachute was 800 feet.

"It's no good, chaps. We're still losing height. All of you — bale out!" Hal's authoritative decree brooked no denial. My navigation watch showed 0053 hours GMT.

"You coming, Skip" asked Bert.

"Yes. No arguments now! We can't hold her — so bale out!"

Behind me Taffy, already in harness, forced a grin as he hooked his 'chute on in front of his chest.

"Come on, man, hurry! You heard what Skip said!" he bawled in my ear as he opened the bulkhead door to the bomb-aimer's hatch.

"Position 35 miles south-west of Mersa Matruh!" I bawled back. The door closed behind him. I then made the same announcement over the intercomm.

Farewells came back, cheerfully spoken:

"Tail-end Charlie baling out, Skip!"

"Second-pilot baling out!"

"Front-gunner joining the Caterpillar Club, Hal!"

"Taffy's already gone," I said, reaching for my harness. Absurdly, I thought of St. George of Merrie England. This shaky-do was like tripping over his lance on the way to the dragon's lair! The starboard engine cleared its throat noisily and began to roar more consistently.

I took a last look round. Still one or two bits and pieces lying about. My Course and Speed Calculator, Sextant, Astro-navigation table-book and parallel rulers only added up to a few pounds, but I reasoned that, in the event, those few pounds could be critical. I shoved them all down the flare-chute. As we were still making a good airspeed the chances of these items getting entangled with descending parachutes was minimal. I was aware that Hal might find himself too low to bale out.

Then I picked up my water-bottle which had slid under the nav. table and looped it to my parachute harness by its webbing-strap.

Finally I kicked out the diamond panel in the floor and, grasping the release handle, let myself down into the night.

6

CHAPTER 1   CATERPILLARS IN THE BLUE

"One and two — and three and four — and five!" I counted. I pulled the handle sometimes called "the ripcord". For an awful fraction of time nothing happened. Then the cords tugged and the silk envelope opened out above me. Something also tugged at my waist but I paid little heed to it at the time.

From the fearful racket of the aeroplane I was plunged into such a silence as I had never before known. I floated downwards, the point of a noiseless cone. Above I could discern no sign of the Wellington — only the star-jewelled tapestry of a September night.

Below me the ground was blurred and shadowy and I strained my eyes to get a glimpse of the terrain I was to land in.

It materialised abruptly. The hump of an enormous bank of shingle rose up and accelerated towards me.

I let myself crumple like a rag doll, muscles relaxed, rolling over on my left side and slithering a fair distance down the slope.

I lay there until all the pebbles had stopped tumbling. Presently, scrambling to my feet, I scrunched around to ensure that I was unharmed. Then I gave thanks to God for my deliverance.

I looked at my navigation watch. It showed five minutes past one o'clock but the glass was cracked, the second-hand motionless. It had broken on the pebbles. Several times I shook it, but all in vain.

Next I felt for my water-bottle. My fingers plucked in vain at the torn end of the broken strap. In that moment of sheer horror I remembered that tug at my waist when the 'chute had opened.

For a few frantic minutes, slithering awkwardly in my flying-boots, I hunted for the bottle, pacing out parallel courses, back and forth, back and forth, scrutinising the shingle in vain.

"Idiot!" I admonished myself at last, speaking aloud, "You're only wasting precious time!"

Again I gazed hopefully at the sky, standing motionless, listening. Perhaps even now I would detect the dark shape of the Wellington, perhaps my ears would catch the splutter of its engine or, fearfully, the terrible din of it crashing onto the desert. But the silence was such as I had never known, could never know anywhere but in a desert. Here at ground level there wasn't even a breath of wind. Standing thus motionless, listening, I fancied I heard the beating of my own heart and the coursing of my own blood.

The names of my crew — I shouted them at the top of my voice. One by one I cried for them, waiting each time until the faint echo had come back from the depths of this wilderness. But of answer there was none. They didn't hear — neither Bert, nor Alf, nor Taffy, nor Bryn, nor Hal.

Little did I know then that, of the five friends for whom I called, there were four I would never see again . . .

CHAPTER 2

Led by a star

I scrambled down to the bottom of the slope. Once there my first task was to bury my rolled-up parachute and my harness together with the broken watch and torn webbing strap. It proved easier than expected for, in scooping up the first handfuls of pebbles I started a mini-avalanche and my discarded kit vanished almost completely into the shingle. It needed only a couple of minutes to complete the process.

Good riddance to that wretched strap for which the stores sergeant had had no replacements in stock. But I was grateful to the cheerfully efficient WAAF staff of the Parachute Section. They regularly checked every 148-Squadron 'chute. It was vital that the silk envelope should be opened out and hung every few weeks. Otherwise the build-up of static could prevent its functioning at the moment of bale-out.

Strange phenomenon — static electricity! I remembered Alf holding the reflector gun-sight bulb in his gloved hand. They were silk gloves and, as he held it, the bulb glowed blue. When I took it from him, it went out!

Thinking of Alf led me to think of the others.

Of Bert, who was forever singing the praises of Coolangatta beach, 70 miles from his home town, Brisbane.

Of Taffy, from Llandovery, full of Welsh fervour and fun.

Of Bryn, whom I didn't know very well because Second Pilots came and went. Alas! they got their captaincy all too soon.

Lastly of Hal whom I knew best of all. We'd swaggered about Blackpool together in our new uniforms, dug trenches together when invasion threatened, and finally, after separate specialist pilot and observer training, crewed up together. We were opposites: Hal's fair hair thin at the temples in contrast to my sleek jet-black mop; he rubicund and moustached, I sallow and clean-shaven; he six years older and very mature while I'd not yet shed the enthusiasms of boyhood.

The other members of my navigation course reached O.T.U. while Hal was still training at Medicine Hat in Canada. But my recovery from the Blackburn Botha crash and subsequent passing-out from Nav. School coincided with Hal's return to England.

We arrived at O.T.U., Harwell on the same day, travelling from Didcot railway station in the same gharry . . .

Such were the reminiscences crowding my spirit in that fleeting moment: my mind's eye saw the crew clearer even than I'd ever seen them in reality.

9

ESCAPE FROM ASCOLI

Again and again I called for them, stirring up whirlpools of sound in the desert night; waiting for their answering cries which never came; for the tiny, rippling echo which sounded farther away each time; for the final, inevitable silence . . .

"If you do bale out in enemy territory, you must bury your parachutes immediately!" That had been the Wing-Co's order. That was why I'd gone to the bottom of the shingle bank where the task could be carried out more effectively. With the passing of time anything buried near the top could easily become exposed again.

Only now did it occur to me that I should first have climbed to the top — the obvious vantage-point from which to seek my comrades. Provided that the enemy were not within earshot or binocular-range!

I mounted to the crest. I found myself on the edge of a wide stony valley bounded by low hills — probably shingle-banks like this one.

One last vain calling of their names before sitting down to consider my predicament.

In the terms of the great explorers this was not deep in the desert — not more than forty miles from the coast. But for the utter emptiness and the absolute silence it could have been the very heart of the Sahara.

To go south, in the direction of distant Siwa Oasis, was therefore out of the question.

I'd no water and little chance of finding any. And I could afford no more time to search for my water-bottle.

The choice was clear:

To walk due north and give myself up to the enemy.

Or to make for Allied lines at El Alamein.

The first option was easier and seemed to offer better hope of immediate survival; the second involved a trek of 140 miles across the Western Desert. Would that be within my powers of endurance and how long was it likely to take me?

I decided on the second option, telling myself that I still could, if necessity demanded, branch north. Whereas a seasoned desert traveller plans his trek from one waterhole to the next, for me the shortest route was the only one possible.

Furthermore it was vital to walk by night and rest during the heat of the day, thus conserving body moisture. An equally important reason was that by night I could navigate by the stars. The Pole Star would give me my direction; the rotation around it of constellations Cassiopeia and The Plough would mark the passage of time.

Allowing for three short breaks, I should be able to walk eight hours a night, starting before sunset and continuing a short time after sunrise. If the going were firm, a 3 miles-per-hour average was feasable, thus making 24 miles in a night. If progress were impeded for any reason, a further hour's walking might be necessary.

At this rate I should reach Allied lines during the sixth night.

CHAPTER 2   LED BY A STAR

I was well-used to walking — it had been my hobby since boyhood. I thought of those long rambles over Epsom Downs, along the Roman road and the Pilgrim's Way out to Colley Hill; or along the River Mole, thence to the top of Box Hill to look down on that lovely panorama of Surrey and its adjoining counties. We often walked more than 24 miles, my dog and I, returning in time for four o'clock tea.

The problem of crossing back into Allied lines involved decisions which I could make only when I reached the El Alamein area. Perhaps I'd be able to make a detour to the south, which, given a supply of water, I would already be doing. But without a water-bottle I had no option but to go due east to begin with. Later I'd alter course south-east, for between Mersa Matruh and El Alamein the coastline slopes down slightly south of east.

As I pondered these matters I was holding that small flat tin familiar to aircrew — the Escape Kit. Now, at last, I opened it. It contained some Horlicks tablets, a tiny saw, some water-purifying tablets, a small rubber bag and a letter printed both in Arabic and English. This was the famous "Ghoolie chit" telling Arabs that here was a British officer who should be treated with respect, for the safe return of whom a substantial reward would be paid. There was also a short vocabulary to enable the "British officer" to utter words like "Saida!" (Greetings!) and "Moya" (Water).

Being "treated with respect" meant not being subjected to the emasculating knife with which certain Arabs were all-too-handy. As to the "substantial reward" there was a chance that more could be obtained from the Germans. It really depended on which side seemed to be having the better of things at the time. So much for euphemisms!

Now was the time for action. It was approximately 0130 hours GMT. Taking note of the positions of the constellations, I got to my feet. Then, turning my left shoulder to the Pole Star, I descended the slope to begin my traverse of this section of the Western Desert.

The plain spread before me like the bed of a huge dried-up lake — mostly stony but with plenty of firm ground to walk on. My boots thudded softly on dirty yellow compacted dust.

For some three hours it was possible to continue in a straight line. Presently, reaching a hill of shingle, I decided to rest a few minutes. So far so good with the first ten miles behind me and no trouble except, perhaps, that my flying-boots were somewhat floppy to walk in.

I'd read somewhere that of all creatures man is least adapted to desert survival: without water or clothing, if exposed to extreme temperatures, he will perish in only one day. My own clothing was scant — just a pair of K.D. shorts and a torn K.D. shirt; but in September, within fifty miles of the sea, the temperatures, I thought, were not likely to exceed 100 degrees Fahrenheit. Furthermore every step would take me, albeit obliquely, nearer to the coast.

On the credit side also was my sallow complexion which betokened natural-protective oils, and my ability to sleep anywhere, anytime. I never

11

doubted that I could sleep the hot day through, but prayed that I might find some sort of shelter around daybreak.

Thereupon I set off again, making for the valley on my right and glancing back frequently at the Pole Star. After about a quarter of an hour I was able to resume my easterly course.

Now I was striding through a wadi where the ground took on the shape of rippling water. There were other shapes to be seen too — wheel-ruts! I could only guess at how long ago trucks had passed this way. It needed a Sherlock Holmes to determine whether it were two days, two months, two years or two decades. Had it been two hours, or even four, the sound of the engines would surely have reached my ears. Had the trucks belonged to some explorer long ago? or to Rommel's army? or to Wavell's? or to Montgomery's? How wonderful it would be, I thought, to meet up with a Long-Range Desert Group unit probing behind enemy lines!

But there was no sound other than my own footsteps, no movement other than my own vague moon-shadow going on ahead of me; no bird of the night; no animal, reptile or insect. It was only in the canopy of the heavens, drawn strangely close above my head, that there was perceptible motion — Cassiopaea and The Plough on their predestined course around Polaris; and, more dramatically, now and again the searing glow of a shooting star in its final agony.

Now I was crossing a broad track, likewise wheel-rutted, running north-south. I guessed that this would be the way down to Siwa Oasis some 200 miles to the south-west, and I thought of the many hopeful travellers who might have gone this way. Presently the stony ground closed in again and my flying-boots chafed me more painfully at every step.

I tried walking barefoot but the stones bruised my feet. Nothing for it, therefore, but to limp on in the torturesome boots, my pace sadly reduced.

It was only then that I became aware of a presence beside me, not visible, not physically definable, but living and real. It was like walking with an old and trusted friend, chatting away with no need to look at him to know his reactions. I spoke aloud, my voice an unrecognisable croak.

"God, these boots are killing me!" Then I thought that maybe I should have used the word "God," with a little more reverence. I apologised and humbly prayed, thinking through the Lord's Prayer as I continued to go forward.

"I'm not going to make it in these boots. D'you think I ought to go north and give myself up?"

It seemed to me that my companion shook his head.

It was as though his hand was grasping mine, urging me on.

Already delicate pastel colours were showing above the flat horizon ahead. The new day was rising to meet me. Light spread magically across the land. Little things that I'd not otherwise have noticed suddenly stood out sharp and clear: larger stones, occasional ruts and, not fifty yards ahead something white about the size of a man's hand. It was gently fluttering.

CHAPTER 2   LED BY A STAR

I hurried forward and picked it up — a scrap of newspaper! It had been torn from the title page for in large black type were printed the words "Der Kamp"! I looked in vain for the date. Then I scanned the plain carefully for any sign of its Afrika Korps readers.

But there was nobody. The desert seemed as empty of life as ever.

CHAPTER 3

Feet and bones

About a mile to the south a huddle of red sandstone rocks stood out against the undulating skyline. As I branched south-east towards them the sun appeared quite abruptly. Instinctively I raised my left hand to shield my eyes, and, turning away slightly, my eye caught the glint of an object close to my feet.

I stooped and picked it up — a tin of pineapple with a faded English label. I shook it and heard liquid lapping inside. I was sorely tempted to open it with the escape saw, but, realising the dangers of drinking from such a tin, threw it down again.

It was not until I was within a hundred yards of the rocks that I noticed, scattered in their shadow, a miscellany of objects: a leather strap, broken crockery, charred embers and a cloth which on closer inspection turned out to be a blanket reeking of camel. Not too long ago Arabs had camped here.

Weary now after 25 miles, I was about to lie down on the blanket in the shelter of an egg-shaped rock when my companion exclaimed:

"Wait a bit! Better have a good look round first!"

"O.K., if you say so!"

I let go of the blanket and made my way among the stones, eventually reaching the far side of the two largest boulders.

"There's nobody about," I declared.

"Use your eyes, Ken!"

Then I saw it, close up against the rock — a brown plimsoll! I picked it up. It was slit across the instep but the sole was good.

I pulled off a flying-boot and tried it on. It fitted perfectly!

"You see!" chuckled my companion, "Now find its mate."

I hobbled about hopefully and there, sure enough, twenty yards to my left, was its partner, also slit across the top!

I put it on, then hid my discarded flying-boots among the stones.

"Thanks a million, friend!"

"No trouble, Ken. You may go to sleep on your blanket now.'

Accordingly I wrapped the camel-cloth around me marvelling that, in spite of the odour, there wasn't a fly to be seen. This was a dead place, yet I'd heard tell that, even in the most arid desert, life was lying dormant ready to burgeon forth at the first whisper of rain.

I awoke to a blaze of heat, the sun directly overhead and shade non-existent. The rock beside me was like a furnace.

15

I edged round to a patch of ground nicely situated to catch the afternoon shadow when it came and to avoid the fiercesome reverberations of heat emanating from the rock.

Then, against all the odds, by relaxing my muscles and lying completely still, I slept through the torrid afternoon. I came to myself to behold the gigantic orange sun poised above the hills from which I'd started my journey.

Before getting to my feet I scanned the area cautiously. Perhaps there was life which, lacking the practised eye of the naturalist, I was unable to detect — sand-grouse for example marvellously camouflaged, or jerboas. I realised that, if any such creatures inhabited this place, they too would only be active by night.

Even at this hour the whole land was still trembling in a feverish heat-shimmer; and, if there had been any animal movement, it would have been almost impossible to detect it.

Standing now, I supported myself against the nearest boulder. I drew back immediately for the rock was still oven-hot! I must have underestimated the September temperatures!

With the setting sun behind me I was about to continue the long walk.

"What about the blanket?" queried my companion.

"I'm leaving it exactly where I found it." My voice was scarcely audible.

"Good decision!"

I took a step forward but my companion restrained me.

"Hang on a bit, Ken. Think! You walked all last night without water, you know."

"No problem. I'd had something to drink in the aircraft and it wasn't a whole night anyway.'

"Fair enough! But you must think about it now. Your throat's drier than an old bone!"

Water! Hitherto I'd managed to concentrate on other things, but now, after the day's heat, my craving thirst could no longer be ignored.

Quite unbidden, past scenes came back to me: a spring bubbling out of the red sandstone not far from Exeter; a waterfall on the wooded Snowdon mountainside: the Dorset Stour ambling through the meadows; above all, closer at hand in Cairo, the big glass cylinder of iced water in the New Zealand Club. Only two days previously I'd hitch-hiked the forty kilometres just to have a drink from it.

How we all grumbled about the heavily-chlorinated liquid available at camp yet how glad I'd have been for a sip of it now!

My hand had strayed to the back pocket of my shorts to extract the Escape Kit tin. I now realised that, if I were to survive, I could not afford to waste any moisture from my own body. Water is life, and, from whatever source, every drop of it precious.

I had lost much from daytime perspiration. However by resting I had reduced that loss as far as was possible.

It behoved me likewise to conserve the water element of bladder excretion.

16

CHAPTER 3   FEET AND BONES

I'd heard somewhere that the water-content of urine is around 95%. For the 5% impurities I'd have to trust the efficacy of the water-purifying tablets.

I dropped a tablet in first and, after filling the bag, waited a few minutes. The resulting brew was as unpalatable as the liquid available to us at camp, but it eased the dryness of my throat and moistened my skin.

Turned inside out, the bag dried in a few seconds and, replacing it in the tin and the tin in my back pocket, I set forth again for El Alamein. It was the night of 20/21st September, 1942.

The way, although stony in places, was much easier than on the previous night, the plimsolls a joy to walk in. My footsteps were light, and I moved quickly and noiselessly across the plain, estimating my speed at nearly 5 miles per hour!

There wasn't a breath of wind. The stillness was absolute. Because of this I felt the presence of my companion as strongly as ever. The words came back to me:

"Be still then, and know that I am God."

Shorn of the trappings of civilisation, I began to comprehend the meaning of silence.

I saw no sign of life, neither in the white and grey stones of the plateau nor among the rocks lurking down there to my south. Perhaps I was going too quickly to notice!

I didn't stop until Cassiopeia and The Plough had taken up the positions they had occupied at the moment of my setting out the previous night, that is, 0130 hours G.M.T. — three-and-a-half hours' walking at nearly 5 miles per hour meant that I'd covered a further 17 miles, making 42 in the 24 hours. With any luck I should manage another 25 miles before my day's rest, making a round total of 70 miles behind me — just half the distance to El Alamein!

Having for the second time performed the water-purifying routine, I popped a Horlicks tablet into my mouth. Sucking it would perhaps ease my parched throat.

I was quickly disillusioned. The sweetness only aggravated my growing thirst and I spat it out in disgust. I realised that, until I was able to drink in any quantity, taking food was sheer folly.

However I was encouraged by the progress I'd already made and, refreshed by the cool night air, I continued on my way. Now I was crossing a wadi whose pebbles reflected the light of a million stars, whose tiny shadows were cast by the moon growing out of its first quarter.

My course was slightly south of east — in compass terms about 110 degrees — that is, parallel to the slope of the coastline between Mersa Matruh and El Alamein. Soon the land billowed up again into low hills while the army of rocks seemed to be closing in on my right.

Once or twice I stopped deliberately to listen and to look about me. It was on one such occasion that I distinguished a familiar sound — the homely throbbing of Pegasus engines. It grew in quick crescendo as the Wimpy

17

passed overhead a mile or two to my north. I scanned the sky in vain until that pulsing rhythm had completely faded into the distance towards the Bay of Sollum.

I wondered if it was a 148-Squadron Wellington and, if so, who was crewing it.

It was indeed an incongruous situation. At one moment there was the illusion of being deep in the Sahara; at the next the trappings of civilisation loomed close — a camp newspaper, a tin of pineapple juice, some of my friends just a mile-and-a-half above me riding the sky in a Wellington.

I went forward more warily now lest, in my eagerness to keep up a good pace, I should stumble unawares upon the enemy.

In fact I became over-cautious, often dropping flat upon the ground because I thought I'd detected something moving among the boulders, or the glint of a rifle, or a shadow that was more than a shadow.

During the next hour I slowed down considerably, but after a number of false alarms I began to strike the happy medium, probably 3 to 4 m.p.h. over the flat, less when ascending the slopes.

From the crest of each hill I half-expected to catch a glimpse of the sea, yet realised that it was still too far away. Doubtless that Wellington crew had been able to make out the coastline.

For me the vista was always a wide stony plain with low hills to the east and now a rocky ledge to the south.

Nowhere was there any green thing nor any sign of water. My throat, indeed all my body was burning. It was a craving that was more than the want of a drink. I wondered what would become of me if I didn't soon find water.

It seemed that my companion nudged me, drawing my attention to something on the ground to my right.

I went over to it hopefully, then stopped in horror: it was a skeleton, white and sun-bleached.

The leg-bones were long and the rib-cage wide too big for a human being. At last discovering the skull, I knew it for the skeleton of a camel.

There were no other remains or debris but not far from the skull I beheld a circle of large stones. Closer examination revealed a rusty wire-mesh grating. My heart leapt. I'd found a water-hole!

But as I gazed into the depths of it, my joy gave way to black despair. Without rope or bucket I had no way of fetching up the water. I cried aloud in frustration.

My companion brought me to my senses, directing my attention to the pebbles at my feet.

I chose one and dropped it through the grating. I counted two seconds before I heard, not a splash but its impact upon other pebbles. At a rough estimate the hole was over 80 feet deep.

Even as I came to this conclusion, the first sign of life appeared before my eyes. A swarm of tiny gnats rose angrily above the grating, hovering

18

there briefly before descending to eke out their final hours on the diminishing moisture.

Their lives, like all life on this planet, was precisely measured in terms of the amount of water available.

It suddenly dawned on me that, in studying the desert, I was looking in upon the beginning of the end of the world.

In the scheme of Creation whether I, personally, lived or died at this time was of little consequence. And of how much consequence was the war? I wondered. Perhaps, in standing against tyranny, we were doing something to aid the divine purpose. If I now decided to go north and give myself up, I'd be helping the cause of the thugs who sought to intimidate their fellow-men — the persecutors of the human spirit.

I was sorely tempted but, sensing the stern disapproval of my companion, I turned my face again to the east and trudged on towards the morning . . .

CHAPTER 4

Stones and bullets

The light came sooner than I had expected, but nowhere in that wilderness could I discern any convenient place to shelter for the day.

The best I could find was a bank of loose shingle at the bottom of which was a small patch of soft fine dust. There I curled up like an animal and, from sheer exhaustion, immediately fell fast asleep . . .

When I came to myself the heat of the day had passed over me and into me: my body was a raging furnace, my temples loudly throbbing and every dried-up part of me yearning for water.

The rubber bag, when I used it, gave me back but a few paltry drops, for my bladder also was dry. However many pints had been wasted in sweat that day I could only guess at.

"Don't despair, Ken. You covered a good distance last night — at least 35 miles. That's 60 miles since you started."

My companion was very real. Whether I was listening to a voice within me or beside me I didn't know, only that, like the rest of Creation, it was there.

I staggered to my feet, really in no condition to walk even one of the eighty miles remaining, but it seemed that my companion was taking my hand and leading me forward in spite of myself.

I rested frequently but he never let me completely give in to my utter weariness, raising me to my feet and urging me on.

My progress was now absymally slow and, as the rocky ground to my south was closing in on me, I chose the easier terrain and walked due east. Thus the coastline was all the time sloping down to meet me.

This night slipped away strangely quickly, for during the last of my rest periods sleep overcame me so completely that I must have lain on the ground at least a couple of hours.

I awoke to the gentle first light. As I sat up I noticed that the stones around me were glistening. I shouted for very joy. They were wet with dew! The precious droplets had condensed out of the cool night air.

Longtime I went from one to another of the larger stones sucking up the Heavensent water. When the dryness had gone from my throat I stripped off shirt and shorts to moisten my whole body, rubbing it with smaller wet stones.

At long last miraculously refreshed, I went on my way at my old jaunty pace. To compensate for my slow progress on this night of 21st/22nd

21

September, I'd have to continue awhile after sunrise. I estimated ruefully that so far the night's tally was scarcely ten miles . . .

I didn't see the jeep until the first rays of the sun were streaming over the hill in front of me.

I dropped flat to the ground and lay a long while observing it. It was stationary at the foot of a twenty-foot-high ledge. No sound of an engine, no sign of driver or occupants and, as the light grew, it showed up as nothing more than a wreck among the boulders.

Cautiously on elbows and knees I approached it. A British jeep, its side hugely dented, its radiator smashed. Of tyres there were none. Jacked up on a couple of big stones, it leaned at a drunken angle on its broken front axle. I hardly dared imagine the circumstances which had caused it to be driven full tilt into those rocks.

Perhaps the wheels had been taken by the same Arabs whose encampment I'd found. If so, I reckoned the plimsolls a fair exchange!

By now the sun was full risen and the day's heat returning. It would be folly to walk much further in spite of the fact that this night I'd made but little progress — only about 15 miles.

Throwing caution aside, I climbed to the top of the cliff and looked about me for some place to shelter for the day.

I was rewarded by the sight of a ready-made "hide" of oil-drums and groundsheets not a hundred yards away to the south-east. Like the hulk of the jeep it was obviously deserted.

I descended with all haste and soon reached the hide. The ground here was free of pebbles but the place was littered with spent .303 cartridge-cases. It must once have served as a machine-gun post and, thinking also of the wrecked jeep, I guessed there had been a scrap here.

The large groundsheet, conveniently draped over the oil-drums, needed no re-arranging. I crawled underneath it and, again curling into a little ball, fell asleep . . .

It was a dream about the garden of my boyhood where the bees were loud in the honeysuckle and the heavy-laden pear-tree branches traced a pattern against the sky.

But the humming grew louder and one of the pears took on a definitive triangular shape and seemed rapidly to be growing bigger. I opened my eyes and perceived, from between the oil-drums and below the groundsheet, a plane swooping towards me. It was an enemy spotter plane — a Fieseler-Storch!

I dared not move a muscle, watching it in fascinated horror as one may watch a cobra poised to strike.

It struck all right! It strafed the hide with a torrent of bullets. They hissed about my ears, rattling into the oil-drums and tearing holes in the groundsheet.

I closed my eyes and prayed. The roar of the engine receded, faded to a hum and, as it finally died away I looked at the aircraft again. It was already a mere dot in the morning sky, fast-disappearing northwards.

Yet again I had to give thanks for a miracle. There were four holes in the groundsheet. There must have been many more in the oil-drums but, judging that the hide could even now be under binocular surveillance, I didn't go out to look.

Amazingly, nowhere on my body was there a scratch! True, my knees and elbows were somewhat chafed from the times when I'd lain flat and crawled across the stones. Yet of the 50 or 60 rounds fired at the hide not one had struck me!

I decided that neither pilot nor observer had seen me. They'd just been amusing themselves in a light-hearted way with a spot of target-practice.

I wondered then how the others were faring — Taffy, Bert, Alf, Bryn and Hal. Strange that I had not seen any of them making in the same direction as I! Taffy, Bert, Alf and Bryn had, I believe, all baled out before me and could be together. Probably Hal too, would be on his own; and, being the man he was, surely he, too, would be making for the Allied lines.

I reflected on my long walk during the second night. Doubtless I had over-estimated the distance covered, for, although my maximum pace was approaching 5 miles per hour, my average was considerably less. However, taking all in all, I'd now certainly travelled some 70 miles, about half-way! That put me 40-45 miles due south of the headland Ras el Kanayis on this the twenty-second day of September.

Curious coincidence! It was on the 22nd June that we had taken off from Gibraltar in Wellington HF832 briefed to make landfall at Ras el Kanayis. At that time Malta was under almost-continuous aerial bombardment. Therefore we had to fly to Cairo in one hop — some task for a Wellington! To make this possible we carried overload fuel tanks instead of a front gunner. Alf was left behind to come on later by sea or maybe in another aircraft.

To say that we "took off" from the short Gibraltar runway was an overstatement. At full throttle we somehow struggled clear of it, immediately sinking to wave-hopping height. Fortunately the Med. was placid. If there had been any waves they would surely have washed us down into the "drink"!

We continued at this height for sixty agonising minutes, praying that no surface vessel would cross our track.

At the end of the hour we switched over to main fuel tanks, extremely careful to turn the cocks in the correct sequence. A mistake would have brought us disaster.

The Pegasus engines had coughed encouragingly — cleared their throats as it were — and set about taking us up into the sky.

"Hullo there, Skip! Permission to dry me feet now?" wise-cracked Bert from the rear turret.

23

"Permission granted, but close the door please!" Hal had retorted, adding, "We're flying on petrol again now the cleaning fluid's all used up!"

That trip counted as our first op.. We'd left Gib. at 1545 hours G.M.T. on 22nd June and would not land in Cairo until 0453 hours G.M.T. the following morning. As navigator I had to work continuously for thirteen hours and eight minutes! Nor could I afford the luxury of one mistake.

With the sextant I took sites of my favourite stars, Dubhe, Arcturus, Rigel and the rest, using Polaris to keep a constant check on our latitude to confirm our safe distance from the North African coast. In the early stages this was visible so that, with hand-held compass I made running fixes from coastal lights. When at last we'd gained height I was also able to study the wind-lanes on the surface of the water. Over and over again I calculated the wind velocity; but when Taffy gave me a radio bearing, I roared with laughter. Like so many wireless bearings it was hopelessly inaccurate.

Ten hours out of sight of land put dead-reckoning to the supreme test. Taffy, Hal and second-pilot Pete took turns in sleeping. This was most encouraging and proved their faith in me.

Bert and I kept intercomm. silence except for an occasional sally such as, "Don't suppose you've any idea where we are, Ken?"

"I can tell you exactly, Digger. Europe to the left, Africa to the right and Asia straight ahead.' . . .

When at last within ten minutes of E.T.A. at Ras el Kanayis, he'd cried out excitedly:

"Ken, there's a coastal light over to port!"

This caused general unrest and Taffy muttered something about Crete. I tried to calm them.

"It's not like Australia, Bert. In these latitudes stars rise in the east. Actually that 'coastal light's' a planet!"

At that moment Pete's cultured voice chimed in:

"I can see Ras el Kanayis. It's straight ahead."

The noises of congratulation from the crew were capped by Hal's quiet observation as we crossed the coast:

"We're dead on E.T.A., Ken. Well done!"

I loaded a red-green cartridge into the Verey pistol while Hal pushed the stick forward. We'd been briefed to circle Kanayis at 4000 feet, identifying ourselves by firing the colours of the day. At this hour of the morning these were red-green.

I could discern some movement on the ground and imagined our army boys giving us a wave and maybe a cheer.

I opened the astrodome and fired the pistol. The red-and-green ribbons hung prettily side by side, then quickly faded into smoke-plumes.

Whoever was responsible down below had probably mislaid the pistol, or the cartridges, or himself because we received no answer.

We made another circuit before setting course for Cairo West aerodrome.

The de-briefing officer was obviously surprised that we'd arrived at all.

CHAPTER 4 STONES AND BULLETS

When we complained about the lack of response at Ras el Kanayis he remarked casually:

"That's quite understandable. You see, our chaps pulled out yesterday. The Germans are there now!'...

Such were my thoughts as I drifted into sleep beside the bullet-pocked oil-drums.

I awoke shortly before sunset. My throat was painfully dry and there seemed to be a huge lump in it. Nevertheless I was encouraged by the prospect of dew the following morning.

On the other hand I would henceforward have to be more alert than ever, all senses keyed up for the slightest sign of the enemy; for footsteps or footprints; for the hum of an engine, the rattle of stones, the click of a safety-catch; for any hint of landmines.

I consulted my companion.

"You'd have had no chance in those flying-boots!" he laughed, "Now with the plimsolls you can move like a shadow — you'll see. Just trust me! I'll see you through."

As he spoke the sun dipped below the hills. Committing myself to his care, I scrambled to my feet to continue my trek this night of 22nd/23rd September.

Contrary to all my fears it proved an uneventful night's walking unless the insufferable torture of growing thirst be counted as an event.

In spite of all efforts to conserve body-moisture, in spite of the dew the previous morning, the dry lump in my throat began to choke me and my whole craving body was weakening at every step.

Rest-periods were times of near-collapse. To my consternation the way was becoming less and less stony and I wondered if I could really survive this night.

"Trust me!" reiterated my companion.

Forward then unsteadily across the expanse of fine dust, quite unexcited by the first puny patch of scrub. "Resting" there, then on and on, mechanically putting one foot in front of the other.

Cassiopaea and the Plough had rotated to show about four o'clock in the morning when — praise be! — I came once more to stony ground.

Millions of stones glistening in the light of the stars and of the half-disc of a moon.

If I'd had tears to shed I would have wept.

Crazily I pressed stone after stone against the pores of my skin. At last, finding slabs covered in dew, I threw all caution aside and hastened from one to another, avidly sucking the water.

I must have spent all of quarter of an hour in this way before I noticed that many of the stones were symmetrical and bore evidence of having been shaped by human hand. I saw paving stones, the footings of walls, a couple of truncated columns and parts of columns lying on their sides — apparently the remains of one of the many Roman settlements to be found in North

Africa. In the day of the Caesars the climate here had been more amenable to life.

Traces of irrigation ditches or wells had disappeared, perhaps effaced by war. Some of this destruction could have been recent, a conclusion borne out by my next discovery — a pile of shell-cases.

The dew stood out on them in big droplets. I knelt to sip, an action I immediately regretted. The sulphurous water burnt lips, tongue and throat painfully.

I returned to the pure moisture of the stones, but the acid went on burning me until well into the day.

The sun came up through a copper haze, further proof that I was nearing the coast. I branched south-south-east, the fading Pole Star behind my left shoulder. Desert pebbles were soon replaced by desert dust, making it easy to move silently.

Climbing above the dust-haze, the sun changed from copper to silver, and the air began to shimmer with heat. Ahead of me I spied a cluster of trees and bushes, just the place to shelter for the day.

I quickened my pace, but the nearer I got, the smaller the trees and bushes appeared. When I finally reached the place I found no more than a sparse patch of stunted scrub.

Nevertheless I sought out the most likely-looking bush and lay down underneath it to rest during this the fourth day of my trek — 23rd September.

I couldn't have been there more than two hours when I was awakened by a voice — a voice speaking in German. It sounded close at hand. I held my breath.

"Das ist alles recht und schön!"

That was all. No reply, no comment. Yet the remark must have been addressed to somebody. With extreme caution I looked about me, but saw no one.

"Just a little trick of the desert," explained my companion, "That voice could be miles away!"

The absolute silence closed in again. I laid my head on my arm and slept until the lifeblood of the dying day was red upon the bushes.

CHAPTER 5

The wrong lot

I awoke to the scent of lemon. Had I not slept on the very spot I'd never have discovered it — a microscopic plant with leaves no bigger than full-stops. Rubbing a few between finger and thumb, I breathed deeply the refreshing draught.

Then scrambling to my feet I began to move forward towards low undulating hills. It was the night of 23rd/24th September and by my reckoning I was two days' walking from El Alamein.

Although my legs were heavy and every muscle aching, I forced myself to keep up the pace. The torment of thirst returned and re-doubled; before my eyes I saw the vision of the iced-water decanter in the New Zealand Club. So real it was but always just beyond my reach.

Drums began thumping in my head and my whole body was on fire. "Rest" periods were the times I slumped down, giddy and exhausted. How long they lasted I'll never know — only that the dew came not a moment too soon. Perhaps because I was now nearer the coast, the droplets were more plentiful but I knew that on their own they would not be enough to save me.

I sucked avidly, then rubbed my parched body with the damp pebbles.

At last strength returned to my limbs and, encouraged by my companion, I pressed on again — time to cover another ten miles before daylight.

I rounded the next hill on its south side. Whereupon a sight met my eyes which brought me to an abrupt halt. I dropped to the ground.

I had stumbled upon the enemy landing-strip at Fuqa! Dispersed on the south side were a number of triple-engined Junkers 52 troop-carriers with their strangely-corrugated fuselage.

There was no sign of activity, no taxying aircraft, no revving engines nor could I see any patrolling guards. Ahead of me I distinguished a huddle of tented dug-outs close to the perimeter — a low wall of loosely-heaped stones.

I made for the shelter of this and, scarce daring to breathe, edged forward. After about ten minutes I was abreast of the tents. I stopped and listened. There was no sound of human voice, only a night bird calling in the distance. Doubtless the aircraft and installations would be well-guarded, but just here nobody was waiting up for visitors!

I tiptoed between the huddle of tents, half-expecting to hear a peremptory challenge or the crack of rifle-fire. But there was nothing. Then making my way unchallenged across the stony plain and branching south-south-east I was soon among the folded hills and out-of-sight of the airstrip.

After about five hours the desert flattened out once more and I reverted to an easterly course, keeping my eyes on the ground to avoid the sun's glare.

At the same time I distinctly heard a metallic clatter like the rattle of a chain. Again I lay flat and motionless on the shingle.

The clatter started up again, more prolonged now, followed by the shrieking of metal under stress. Cautiously I raised my head and knew it then for the shunting of goods trucks. This was the coastal railway which ran eastwards from El Daba. It was ahead of me and well to my left.

Presently in the full light of the morning I saw the train quite clearly, a long line of about twenty-five trucks, clanking away eastwards along the Burg el Arab coastline . . .

I crawled forward to conceal myself as best I might behind a tiny patch of scrub. Then all through that scorching day, through the heat-quiver, I watched those trains shuffling up and down the line. I could see that many of the trucks were of the open matchbox-tray type, but had no idea of what goods were being carried.

Yet apart from the busy trains there was no activity whatsoever — no gharries, jeeps, tanks or aircraft. The Fieseler Storch I never saw again.

Now that I was within forty miles of El Alamein my problem was how to penetrate the enemy line. I had only a hazy notion of what such a "line" consisted of. For me, as RAF navigator, lines were straight: that was the way I ruled them on the Mercator's chart. However I doubted if a battle-line was ever straight. Also, allowing for salients, the distance I had to go might be as much as fifty miles or as little as thirty! Furthermore there would not be lines of trenches as in World War I.

I wondered why all was so uncannily quiet. Maybe the enemy already had his binoculars focussed on me.

I hardly dared imagine the obstacles that now lay in my path: mines which I wasn't trained to recognise, hidden gun-positions which I wasn't trained to detect. To make matters worse I had seriously underestimated the distance to the railway.

My companion tried to cheer me:

"At least you've now learnt the trick of moving silently. And you're well-camouflaged with your K.D. shirt and shorts and your sunburned skin."

Crumbs of comfort which didn't solve my problem. But an idea was dawning in my mind. Maybe the best way to go unnoticed was to travel right under the noses of the enemy — in one of those goods trucks! This would take me a few precious miles in the right direction. Because of lack of water, going even a short distance south was out of the question.

Long before sundown I began to crawl forward, examining every inch of the ground for mines, my heart ticking like a geiger-counter at every irregularity, pausing every few yards to draw breath and look about me.

I was startled by a sudden high-pitch screaming overhead. Looking up I

CHAPTER 5   THE WRONG LOT

saw a flight of swifts. They were racing down from the coast, wheeling tight-banked as they dived upon insects beyond my vision. Then at a signal from the leader, the formation turned and vanished as quickly as it had come.

Comforting to see these birds. Perhaps they'd nested in England, perhaps the very ones my love and I had watched in the skies above the Berkshire Downs near Harwell . . .

When the first stars appeared I'd advanced about half a mile and the railway seemed as far away as ever. Furthermore all activity up there had ceased. No longer were any trains to be seen.

Unsteadily I got to my feet. The awesome stillness had returned — nowhere any sign of life.

I picked my way among the stones, searching anxiously for notices reading, "Achtung! Minen!" An hour's tiptoeing brought me to within 300 yards of the railway-line.

I lay down to take stock of the situation before making my final approach.

The railway seemed completely deserted, nor in that widespread table of land could I see any sort of defence installation.

I wriggled forward more cautiously than ever.

It seemed an age before I reached the shallow ditch bordering the track. There I waited awhile, weak from the effort of crawling, letting the blood dry on my knees. They'd taken a pitiful scraping on the stones!

Then as all remained quiet, I mounted onto the single track, turned right and walked along it. My heart leapt when I fancied I saw the sea through a gap between the sandhills.

Presently the embankment, although low and scarcely worthy of the name, became higher on its north side and, realising my folly in walking on the skyline, I scrambled down to the ditch, continuing at a fair pace.

I must have covered as much as a mile before I noticed what I should have spotted long since, what I certainly would have seen had not my eyes been turned towards the coast.

On an eminence on the south side of the track and less than a hundred yards ahead was the top of a round concrete structure.

I halted abruptly, stood on tiptoe the better to observe. Suddenly I realised the peril of my situation. It was a pill-box. I could make out embrasures on the north and west although the entrance was out of my view. Hal and I had manned a similar one at R.A.F. Station, Watchfield in Wiltshire against the expected enemy invasion in 1940.

I threw myself down, lay motionless in the shingle-ditch, listening. Not even the tiniest sound disturbed the brooding silence.

I crawled up the bank, cheek brushing the ground. Then my fingers clawed the end of a railway sleeper. Once again I froze, peering at the forbidding obstacle before me. The pill-box, deathly-white under the moon, stood menacingly between me and the shelter of the rocks. I could detect no protruding gun-muzzle nor indeed any sign that the place was occupied.

29

"But of course there won't be!" I told myself.

"They'll have been watching through binoculars. Now they're only waiting for me to reach point blank range!"

I remembered the advice of the Watchfield sergeant:

"Wait till you can see the whites of their eyes!"

One solitary shot, that's all it would need! I shuddered and, as I did so, lost my grip and slithered noisily down the slope.

I cursed myself for my clumsiness and then again for my presumption in thinking I could walk clean through the ranks of the enemy. Why, oh why, hadn't gone north after bale-out and simply given myself up?

If there were any observers up there, my stealthy antics would certainly earn me a bullet. A third time I cursed myself — this time for not having approached openly.

"Go on, you idiot, get on with it!" The whisper was so real that I instinctively looked up at the speaker. But as before there was nobody to be seen and as I hesitated, I felt as though I'd been given a sudden shove and there I was going over the top. Then I was running and ducking and jinking from side to side. It wasn't of my own volition because the real me was terrified and wondering if I would hear the shot.

Incredibly, without sound or sight of the enemy, I reached the pill-box.

My back tight-pressed against the concrete wall, I strained my ears to catch the rustle of clothing, a suppressed cough maybe or even blatant snoring. Longtime I waited there, my nerves at full stretch.

The stillness was absolute. Perhaps the place was unguarded after all.

I edged round to my left, careful not to dislodge any loose pebbles, stooped low under the west embrasure and moved on to the one facing south. I bowed low again, tiptoed on a few feet. There I stood up, leaning against the wall, plucking up courage. There was still an outside chance that the eastern position was manned.

I offered up a quick prayer, then, throwing caution to the desert breeze, I sprinted the 150 yards southwards to the nearest cluster of rocks.

No shouting behind me, no shooting, no sign of life whatsoever, and in less than half-a-minute I was lying safe behind a large boulder, panting not so much with exhaustion as with relief . . .

Twenty minutes later I was going east again keeping well in the shelter of those rocks.

One thing I knew for certain — they didn't run the trains at night and my crazy notion of hitching a lift could not be put into effect.

With the pill-box out of sight I continued walking normally, judging it no longer necessary to stoop or to crawl . . .

I had just reached the crest of another of those low stony hills when I was startled by the sound of an explosion. It was ahead of me and to my south. Presently I saw flashes, tracer-lines spewing up into the sky and star-shells bursting.

Down there a little bit of Hell was suddenly let loose. The gunfire came

30

to me like the pounding of angry fists: one-two — one-two-three — one-two-three — one-two! Maybe the tanks were lumbering round like heavyweights in the ring. Did every blow betoken the shedding of blood?

That battle, I told myself, must mark the whereabouts of the El Alamein line. I must be almost there. I cried aloud and ran helter-skelter down the slope.

I paused at the bottom, aghast at my own foolhardiness. Luck — or my companion — had guided me out of earshot of the enemy and clear of mines.

What I did find strewn about the area was a debris of wine-bottles, rags of clothing, paper and books and, here and there, discarded rifles. The wine-bottles were mostly beautifully-shaped Chianti with straw-casing and loops for carrying. I picked one up to use, hopefully, as a water-container. Later I picked up a rifle.

The litter continued for about a mile at the end of which distance I threw away the rifle. Carrying it only made the going more wearisome. Anyway, its bolt was missing and I had no ammo. Furthermore I realised that it was folly to appear to be armed. Allies or enemy alike would be inclined to shoot first and ask questions afterwards!

My thirst, which I'd tried so hard to forget now took over my whole being. I knew that dew alone wouldn't save me. It wasn't just my throat: my whole de-hydrated body was desperately weak, craving for moisture. One way or another, my trek was bound to end before the morning.

As for the Chianti bottle, the only means of filling it would be from tap, pump or pool. The chances of that were slender indeed!

I stumbled on. My legs kept on walking while my brain shrieked for rest.

I believe that, if I had rested at that moment, I should never again have got up.

The gunflashes became sporadic and finally ceased.

Fascinated and quite detached, I watched those torn brown plimsolls carrying me steadily forward. The stones were fewer now, the terrain mostly compacted dust, fine as powder.

My companion, still beside me, made no comment, only in this extremity urging me on beyond the limit of my strength.

The guns began to rumble again ever further to the south now and, encouragingly, a long way behind me. The Heavenly clock showed the time as half-past one, The Plough and Cassiopaea situated exactly as at the start of my trek.

Forward I went again. Something stirred a few yards ahead and it was only then I noticed the tented dug-out.

"Chi va là?" The sentry rapped out the challenge and I heard him release the safety-catch on the rifle.

I breathed a sigh of blessed relief. The challenge "Qui va là?" meant that I'd arrived! My smattering of French gave me the translation of "Who goes there?" This must be a Free French outfit.

"Je suis anglais!" I croaked thankfully.

31

ESCAPE FROM ASCOLI

I was immediately surrounded by soldiers, coming up from various dug-outs.

But they were not French. Their uniforms were green, and I realised that I had entered the camp of an advance Italian unit.

For me, the wrong army! . . .

Bleary-eyed, his black hair dishevelled, the capitano faced me across the table.

"Vous êtes soldat français," he declared, buttoning his grey-green tunic.

"No, I'm English." My voice was a whisper and seemed to come from far away.

He shook his head in disbelief. He stroked his stubbly chin with the palm of his hand before picking up a pencil. One of the soldati inquisitively crowding round, placed a blocco noto in front of him.

"Why you talk francese a la sentinella?"

"Because I thought he challenged me in French!" My answer was a distant croak.

He waved aside the soldati, then pointed a grimy accusing finger at me.

"You not look English. I think you French! Toutefois vous êtes soldat?"

The straining of my larynx proved that it was really me saying:

"I'm R.A.F. and my name is 'de Souza'."

"Ecco! 'de Souza' — ça, ce n'est pas anglais."

"And my number is 926093."

As he was noting down this information I saw the caporale coming towards me.

"What grade please?"

His face became blurred and the table started swaying. I didn't reply immediately, whereupon he rapped out:

"Quel grade avez-vous?"

"Sergeant Air-Observer!" I gasped as the tent began to revolve slowly round the captain's grey-green forage-cap. With one hand I gripped the edge of the table, with the other I produced the identity-disc hanging on a cord inside my shirt. He inspected it, let it fall back into place, then eyed me keenly:

"How many days you in the deserto?"

"Six." My voice was farther away than ever.

"Sei giorni senza acqua!" blurted out the caporale, now standing at my elbow, at the same time handing me his water-bottle. His eyes rounded in astonishment as I drank it to the last drop.

The soldiers gathered round me again. I was given another, and then another full water-bottle. I drained both.

The captain nodded approvingly. Then, having recorded my number-rank-name on a memo-pad, he murmured some orders to his men.

A camp-bed was opened out and I sank down upon it gratefully. I then realised that, in all the excitement, no one had searched me. The flat escape-

32

kit tin still nestled in the back pocket of my shorts, quite invisible now as I lay back obviously exhausted.

A sentry was posted at each end of the bed and the other men returned to their quarters. Before sleep overcame me I remember praying that the sentries, facing each other and nervously fingering their rifles, wouldn't accidentally shoot each other! . . .

I awoke to the distant thumping of artillery-fire. Of the two sentries there was no sign. Either the worst had happened or the captain had sent them away.

The caporale again offered his water-bottle of which this time I drank less than a half. Once on my feet I became the focus of an admiring crowd. A prisoner, after all, was something to be proud of! One man, soldato semplice, pointed to my gold wedding-ring, then to himself, saying:

"Anche io sposato!"

That was the signal for the showing of photographs. As I was introduced to all the girlfriends and wives something tugged cruelly at my heart-strings. I turned away close to weeping.

"Ecco sergente, it is for you!"

The sympathetic caporale pressed a comb and case into my hand. The case was of green mock leather and bore the fascist emblem on both its sides.

I thanked him and, turning away again, smuggled the escape-kit saw into the case where it fitted comfortably beside the comb. I was about to comb my hair when we were disturbed by the din of a truck grinding to a halt outside.

The captain re-entered the dug-out.

The Germans come to take you to prison camp!" he announced.

The caporale exclaimed enviously:

"Sergente, for you the war is over!" and, blowing a kiss from the tips of his fingers, added, "Maybe you go to Napoli. Ah! è bellissima — Napoli!"

He obviously believed that, as a prisoner-of-war in Italy, I'd be well-looked-after and have time to enjoy the delights of his country.

I took out the escape-tin and handed it to the captain.

"The Germans will ask if you searched me," I murmured.

He looked confused. The next moment a German officer briskly descended the steps. The two of them conferred briefly. Then, with a satisfied nod, the German pocketed the slip from the memo-pad together with the R.A.F. escape-kit tin.

"Raus!" he barked, glaring at me.

I climbed out of the dug-out to find three members of the Afrika Korps waiting to escort me to the truck.

I was ordered to sit beside the driver in the cab. He was a mountain of a man, and when an armed guard took his place on my right, I was securely wedged in position. With the officer and the other N.C.O. in the back, we set off, jolting across this northern tip of the Libyan Plateau up to the coastal road.

The gravel thinned out and flour-like dust began to rise up through the cab floor. When, with a desperate lurch, the truck, howling like a demon, finally climbed up onto the tarmac, the dust was in our eyes, ears, mouth and teeth, and the hatless driver looked like a coachman in a powdered wig.

I tried to make conversation with the guard but, resolute and steely-eyed, he affected not to hear. Doubtless he had had orders not to speak to the prisoner.

The sun got up above the haze to concentrate its heat on our particular truck. I thought of sausages slow-sizzling in an oven.

Raising dust-clouds, a column of armoured cars clattered by, arrogant-looking Germans, blond and blue-eyed, standing in the hatches. The little roundels above the peaks of their desert caps reminded me of the red-white-and-blue ones on R.A.F. planes.

Then, suddenly, away to my right was the Mediterranean — a vision of tranquillity, aquamarine with distant touches of turquoise and silver. A voice within me seemed to be saying:

"Don't forget, Ken. I'm here. Just have courage."

It would be the bay of Burg el Arab.

To my left beyond the profile of the driver lay, equally tranquil, that shimmering ocean of dust whose horizon was the gravel plain I had crossed on foot in the opposite direction. Ahead, a moving plume of smoke showed that trains were again running on the Daba railway. Above, a couple of Junkers 88s roared in from their sea-patrol on course for Fuqa. Below, the ribbon of road widened, slowed as it widened, lurched about a bit and finally stopped. I noticed a standpipe and tap by the roadside.

"Raus!" Again that ugly word.

We all dismounted to enjoy the midday break. My escort sat in the shade of the truck wolfing bread and sausage and fruit. Then they passed round a bottle of wine, each man taking his gulp.

I was thrown a piece of bread and invited to drink from the tap. The bread was stale and gritty, and the water brackish, but it served.

The road was quiet now and the clanking of trains on the Daba railway was clearly audible. The Junkers 88s had become tiny dots, descending now and circling . . .

Just ten nights ago we had so nearly collided with a Ju 88 near Tobruk — maybe one of those two I was watching.

"Blimey!" had gasped Alf up front.

"Jee — sus!" had shrieked tail-end Bert.

"What was that?" in Cockney tones.

"A bloody You 88, that's what! A couple of feet below us!" in New-South-Wales drawl.

"Keep your eyes peeled, fellers," Hal had said.

The enemy aircrew must have been equally surprised and the Ju 88 hadn't re-appeared.

Likewise in 1940, at Watchfield, I was personally machine-gunned by a

CHAPTER 5   THE WRONG LOT

Junkers 88. A chirpy ground-defence corporal, eager to impress a mere AC2, had just pointed it out to me as a short-nosed Blenheim — one of ours. It had immediately dived at us, spitting bullets which chipped concrete crumbs off the airmen's mess while we lay flat-pressed on the turf.

As we dusted ourselves down afterwards, the chastened Corporal decided that it was one of theirs! . . .

"Schnell! Schnell!" The German officer was flapping his pistol menacingly so I heaved myself back up into the cab.

We churned on through that torrid afternoon, passed Fuqa airfield and Daba peninsula and pulled off the road to refuel. The hillside depot consisted of a cylindrical storage-tank surrounded by stacks of jerry-cans.

Within an hour of restarting we branched north and, as the orange sun hesitated above a distant ridge, we found ourselves entering the prison-of-war camp at Mersa Matruh.

To my left the barbed-wire strands could have been fine-traced in Indian ink, so clear-cut was the silhouette. It made the sun look like a gigantic Chinese lantern.

Behind the wire a working-party of negroes were plodding back to their compound carrying long-handled shovels.

We halted near a group of low white-walled buildings and I was invited to dismount. As I set foot here in Mersa I reflected bitterly that the truck had achieved in one day the journey that had cost me five and a half nights of anguished toil!

Waiting for us was a Chaplin-moustached Italian major rubbing his hands together like an Italian waiter. He later proved to be the Camp Commandant which explains why my German escorting officer saluted him.

They conferred briefly and I saw the escape-tin and the memo-slip change hands once again. Thereupon the German returned to his truck which roared away as soon as he was aboard.

Meanwhile the Commandant ushered me into his office. He sat down gingerly in the ample chair as though it were the hot-plate of a cooker. Indeed I never saw him sit still in that chair: he was constantly wriggling from one cheek onto the other and then back again.

"Sergente de Souza, you airman, yes?"

"Yes," I conceded.

"You 926093?"

"Yes," I replied.

"Pity you shot down in the desert. Where are your friends?"

I occupied the ensuing silent moments by admiring his beautiful polished desk.

"Where you shot down?"

It could have graced the most well-appointed office.

"You walk six days in circles?" with a chuckle.

It was covered in Moroccan leather, swastika-patterned round the perimeter. I cursed myself for having mentioned the "six days".

Suddenly he noticed the comb-case in my shirt-pocket.

"Show me please," he said, holding out his hand. His eyes lit up when he saw the Fascist emblem. 'Si, si! Very nice! Where you get it?"

When I told him, he slid it back to me across the table without examining its contents.

I replaced it in my pocket thinking that, for example, the escape-saw would cut through barbed wire.

He leaned forward intently:

"Sergente, where were you shot down?"

He was on his starboard cheek and smiling obsequiously, more than ever like a waiter. I could have said, "Una cotoletta alla milanese, per favore!" but held my peace.

His smile changed to a scowl as he canted over to port.

"Ver" good. You not say nothing now. You go think about it. We talk again tomorrow." Then, shrill, at the top of his voice, "Alberto!"

The guard strutted into the office and, with the muzzle of his rifle, indicated the way I should go.

As I made my exit the major was busy unwrapping a Horlicks tablet.

CHAPTER 6

A question of nationality

The guard took me to a square canvas tent not far away. As soon as I was inside he began lacing up the flap. In the seconds before I was plunged into darkness I saw that there was no furniture of any kind, just the sand to lie on. Most Italian tents were made of camouflaged groundsheets buttoned together and draped over a frame. Through the buttonholes and at the edges they let in light and fresh air. However this tent was more like a cell, specially designed to keep out the light and to admit as little air as possible.

I nicknamed the comical Italian major "Beppo", reflecting that, with this Charlie-Chaplin features, he has more a clown than a waiter. His moustache was almost identical, and when he was agitated — which was most of the time! — it had the same twitch.

Beppo obviously judged that a spell of solitary confinement would loosen my tongue and that at the next interrogation I'd give him all the information he needed. But I knew I wasn't alone: my companion of the desert was still with me.

To my unvoiced question, the answer was clear:

"Relax Ken, and get some shut-eye!"

Before doing so I prayed that the others might be safe somewhere — Bert and Alf, Taffy and Bryn, and, of course, most trusty of my friends, Hal . . .

I was wakened by Alberto's boot nudging my shoulder. Yawning and rubbing my eyes, I followed him into Beppo's office to participate in Scene 2 of the interrogation comedy.

Beppo greeted me affably:

"Ah, Sergente de Souza, you have good sleep? Please sit down. You like some coffee?"

"No thank you. May I have some water instead?"

"But of course. — Alberto!"

Alberto came charging in again, rifle at the ready. At the captain's request he offered me his water-bottle. But hardly had I put it to my lips than Beppo snapped, "It is enough! — Alberto wrenched it from my grasp, reslung it round his person and, with a clatter of empty coffee-crocks backed out of the room. The pitiful drop of moisture that I'd taken was not enough to ease my parched throat. Beppo clicked open a silver cigarette-case.

"You like cigarette?"

"No, I don't smoke. Thanks all the same."

A pause while he lit up, using his matching silver lighter.

37

"Now we 'ave friendly talk, yes? Just you and I. You answer my simple questions and then go 'ave nice breakfast."

I smiled back at him as engagingly as possible.

"Now you 'ave tell me your name is de Souza, numero 926093 and that you are Sergente-Air-Observer."

I regretted having said that I was an Air Observer but nodded in confirmation.

"de Souza is your cognome. What are your other names? You write them please on this paper."

"Arthur Kenneth," I wrote.

" 'Arthur', it is Italian, yes? Arturo. But 'Kenneth' — what is that?"

"Scottish," I said.

"So you 'ave a Scottish name and an Italian name and a Portuguese name," he grinned, "So what does that make you?"

"Typically English," I explained.

'And the others in your aeroplane? They were also English"

The office was sparsely furnished — apart from the desk, just a few chairs, a cupboard and some files.

"They were not wounded when you shot down?" in solicitous tones, knocking the ash from his cigarette.

The ashtray was quite exquisite, probably Venetian glass.

"Sergente, where you shot down?" The question came at me on a stream of tobacco-smoke.

He bounced from port to starboard and back to port again. Then, looking me in the eyes, he finished his cigarette in silence. I noticed that, as he stubbed it out, his hand was shaking.

At last he put his elbows on the desk and said confidentially, "You understand, I try to help you. Answer my simple questions and there will be no need for interrogation by the Germans."

"You are very kind," I remarked appreciatively, "and I know you are doing your duty . . ."

"Ecco! It is my duty . . ."

"Just as, if you were in my position, you would do your duty. That is, you would give only your number, rank and name."

He shifted to starboard.

"But between us, de Souza, this war is a farce, no? It not really make any difference when you answer questions. It will not change the war. The form will be filled in, put in the file and all forgotten. Nobody will know or care. But, you see, it make life easier for you if you tell me. The Germans, they think you know something more, and they not so kind like me."

Except for occasional lapses in moments of tension, Beppo's English was very commendable. When I told him so he beamed at me in delight. He took up his pen, preparing to write.

"So you will tell me then? Where you shot down?"

I shook my head and the pen clattered back onto the desk. He got up abruptly, strolled over to the window and stood there a long time with his back to me. At last he said, "You like Cairo? It is interesting city, yes?"

He rightly assumed that Allied bomber airfields would not be too far from Cairo.

"So I am told," I rejoined, "You have been there often?"

He shook his finger at me.

"It is for me to ask the questions!" he squeaked, "You laugh in your sleeves, no?"

I glanced down at my bare arms, shrugging my shoulders. He scuttled back to his desk and stood awhile looking at me.

"Where were you based, sergente?"

Through the window I could see a high stone wall surmounted by strands of barbed wire.

At that moment the door was thrown open and a German officer bustled in. He was carrying a sheaf of papers. He nodded curtly to Beppo and sat down in the deskchair. The Italian hovered uncertainly a moment before taking his departure.

My new inquisitor appeared to be reading from his notes.

"You are 926093 Sergeant de Souza, air-observer, Wellington bomber squadron based in the Delta area. That is correct?"

He looked up sharply, fixing me with his penetrating grey eyes.

"My number, rank and name are correct," I confirmed.

"Sergeant de Souza, we know what is correct, so I tell you, hein? You will be happy to know your crew is safe and prisoners-of-war like yourself. And we have found your Wellington bomber."

I thought immediately of the spotter aircraft, the Fieseler-Storch. A German observer, equipped with binoculars, might well have located the Wellington. Yet it was strange that, in the silence of the desert, I'd not heard it crash.

Then again, if my friends had really been captured, he would mention their names.

"You are not happy that your crew is safe?"

"I'm only happy to tell you my number, rank and name," I reiterated, "as you yourself would do if you were a prisoner-of-war."

He never for one moment took his eyes off me, remarking quietly:

"There may be times when it is wise to put our own personal safety and well-being before that of our country." A menacing pause, then, "Only one more thing, sergeant: when will come the great British attack? German Intelligence knows that it is to be soon."

I shrugged my shoulders.

"It will not make any difference of course. The war is almost over. Already the victorious German army have entered Stalingrad. After the defeat of Russia, England will quickly accept peace terms . . . So — the offensive at Alamein — it is to be September 30th, no?"

Privately I doubted whether Monty would choose that date for it was our third wedding anniversary!

"I'm only an airman and I just don't know," I replied, adding, "All that I do know is that it will be very powerful. It will sweep your armies right out of Africa and prove the turning-point of the war!"

I regretted the words as soon as I had uttered them.

He stood up, his face darkening with anger, his fists clenched. Then, gaining control of himself, he said coldly:

"Insolence will not help you. However we will say no more now. Perhaps later you will reply sensibly to our questions!"

He gathered up his papers, turned on his heel and made his exit.

That was the cue for Alberto to march me away to the prison-camp compound. Outside the door we passed Beppo who looked at me pityingly and shook his head. He'd done his utmost to spare me the rigours of German interrogation.

I made my way between high barbed-wire fences, stranded and rolled. The outer perimeter was on my left, the compound on my right.

The negroes, setting out for another day's toil, were shuffling by outside the wire. In their wake strolled a couple of Germans armed with automatic weapons.

One of the negroes smiled at me furtively. Then suddenly, with a powerful throw, he slung his water-bottle over the wire so that it landed at my feet. As I gratefully picked it up, the nearest German guard was screaming at him angrily. He just grinned at me and shuffled on.

I was deeply touched by this act of self-sacrifice by a man whom I'd never met before, would probably never meet again, of different race, of different religion. Alberto for his part pretended not to notice, concentrating on opening the barbed-wire gate.

There was only one tent in the compound. Alberto waved me towards it, closed the gate and took up sentry-position outside. I was filled with sudden hope. Maybe I was about to be re-united with my crew. I drew back the flap and entered.

Coming in from the glare of the morning sun I was momentarily blinded and all but tripped over the crossed legs of a Sikh! He was sitting, turban on lap, combing his long beautiful hair. He looked up at me, grinned hugely from behind an ample beard, then put his hands together in greeting. I too put my hands together and courteously inclined my head. Thereupon he again took the comb out of his hair and serenely went on with his combing.

As I carefully stepped round him another smiling face appeared out of the gloom and a welcoming hand shot forward. I shook it, identifying its owner as a lithe, friendly-looking man, not as dark-skinned as the Sikh but slightly darker than myself.

"You English?" he asked.

I nodded.

"I Gurkha!" he told me proudly, pumping my hand.

CHAPTER 6   A QUESTION OF NATIONALITY

That was the sum total of all the conversation we ever had, except that he got to calling me "Tommy" because all British fighting-men were Tommies, and I addressed him as "Johnny" because Johnny Gurkha was one of the most respected of all our allies.

A strange phenomenon, this close communion that men may have without the aid of spoken language. Johnny and I had so much in common, laughing a lot together and communicating by means of looks and gestures.

He took me round the compound like a squire showing me his estate, pointing out the interesting features — a gap in the barbed wire here, a sentry-box there, a minefield at such-and-such a point outside the wall, and, most importantly, the square pit which had been dug for the easement of Nature's wants. Beside it was a heap of lime from which shovelfuls had already been thrown into the bottom.

Outside the wire not far from the commandant's office we saw a small concrete-block building whose door and window must have been on the opposite side. Johnny performed an hilarious digging mime to suggest that it might be a store for shovels.

As we returned to the tent, the Sikh, full-turbanned now, was making his way towards the pit. Completely ignoring Johnny, he bestowed upon me a respectful hands-together greeting before hurrying on his way.

In the short time I was with them I noticed that the two Indians barely tolerated each other, avoiding each other's company as much as possible. I sensed a traditional enmity simmering below the surface.

CHAPTER 7

Red double-cross

I was better fed by the enemy at Mersa than at any other P.O.W. camp. Thick vegetable soups or stews were served daily in round Italian-issue messtins, and water from the compound tap, though warm, was always palatable.

Towards the evening of that first day — the seventh since my bale-out — I was called for further questioning. This guard was short, dark, plump and sparsely bearded, the enthusiastic Alberto presumably off-duty.

I followed the slouching figure into Beppo's office, thinking that, in the interests of Axis security, it was he who should have been walking behind! In other circumstances he could have looked round and found me gone! Or, had I been the physical type, he might not have had the time to do so!

Beppo was at his most comic.

"Sergente, I am 'appy to see you already looking in better health. They take good care of you?"

"The cuisine is excellent!" I complimented him as he wobbled in his chair.

"But why you always laugh in your sleeves? This time you tell me some answers, yes? It is not a game, sergente, and it is better that you tell me. The Germans will make you tell them, you know."

He paused hopefully.

"It all depends on the questions," I said.

"Then sergente, where you based?" almost jumping out of his chair at this hint of co-operation.

"The German officer told me he already knows that," I informed him.

"What kind of aeroplane you fly?"

"He says he knows that too."

"Your target?"

"Yes," I said, "he reckons he knows it all."

He slewed to starboard and his little moustache twitched irritably.

"Then I ask you when will come the British push?"

I shrugged my shoulders.

I thought of those attacks we had made on Rommel's armour at the end of August and beginning of September — 250-pounders with a leavening of 40-pound anti-personnel bombs. We had played our part in the first-ever victory over the "invincible" German Army. At Alam Halfa the Desert Fox

43

had been out-generalled, his Afrika Korps outfought. I was proud to have been there at the turning of the tide.

He waggled his finger at me.

"You no answer! The British push . . ."

"Will sweep your lot right out of Africa!" Once again the words came tumbling out of their own accord. Like the German officer he leapt to his feet.

"Go now!" he spluttered, "I ask you no more question! Via! Via!" And he pointed dramatically at the door. "Remember, all you prisoners, you stay inside the tent at night! You go outside, you be shot!"

I found Sloucher waiting to conduct me back to the compound.

Beppo's emotion, I suspected, was more of fear than rage. Perhaps he too was having doubts about ultimate Axis victory . . .

Daylight was beginning to fade when the returning negro working-party trudged wearily by on the other side of the wire. I scrutinised every face, but all in vain. My Good Samaritan was no longer among them.

Softly Johnny began humming a Nepalese lullaby and the Sikh's comb took up the rhythm of it.

Watching the brightening stars through the open tent-flap I fell sound asleep . . .

It must have been towards midnight when we were awakened by a sudden scream! Then another and another and another! Screams of terror!

The Sikh sat up, rubbing his eyes while Johnny sprang to his feet and peered out of the tent. With difficulty I restrained him from going outside.

The screams continued, interspersed with sobbing. The Sikh rolled his eyes and Johnny's hand moved instinctively to his belt, feeling for the kukri knife that wasn't there any more. He pointed towards the concrete store-hut. As he did so we distinguished the murmur of voices. The voice that had cried out was whimpering as if in pain. Then it crescendoed to a shriek:

"No! No! No! No!"

Immediately there followed a shot — just one solitary shot . . .

The ensuing silence was, for me, a whole age of bitterness and sadness.

We were never to know, or have proof of, what seemed to have been a brutal act of torture culminating in cold-blooded murder.

Be that as it may, I never saw my Good Samaritan again.

The following morning, after we had amply breakfasted, the Sikh was taken from us, either for further interrogation or to join other Sikh POW's. I'd only known him briefly — that tall, turbanned soldier whose flashing white teeth were as brilliant as his flashing black eyes. In his leave-taking he performed those familiar gestures — pressing together his hands and inclining his head.

Yet another comrade I was never to meet again . . .

Johnny and I took a turn round the compound, paying special attention to the squat white building as we passed nearby. The blank concrete walls revealed no clue to the happenings of the night.

On our return to the tent Johnny produced a large red sash which he carefully folded. He gave it to me indicating that I was to use it as a pillow. It was a welcome gift because, comb as I might, I'd never rid my hair of the powdery sand picked up while sleeping on the ground.

I was washing my hair under the tap when Alberto arrived to take me for further questioning. Johnny winked at me encouragingly as I departed.

Gloomy and lacking his previous élan, Alberto ushered me back into the Commandant's office.

The German intelligence officer was sitting at the desk consulting his papers. Beppo stood beside him looking over his shoulder. (Would the Signore prefer osso buco or pollo arrosto?) Both feigned not to notice me.

From where I stood I had a clear view of the other wall of the little concrete building. The key was still in the lock of the small green door. As for the window, it was no more than a narrow slit.

"Good morning, sergeant, I trust you spent a comfortable night?" The German acknowledged my presence in the friendliest manner.

"I slept like a top," I lied, noticing that he too glanced momentarily out of the window. Could the night's barbaric drama have been enacted especially for the benefit of those about to be interrogated? I would never know, but I feared the worst.

"That is very good. You are also very lucky because today comes the Red Cross officer. We expect him any minute and we shall allow you to speak with him."

I let my delight be apparent, but hid my doubts.

It was indeed no more than a minute before we heard a vehicle draw up outside. The slam of a car door, a few gutteral words, and in strode the Red Cross officer respendent in his Red Cross uniform, with Red Cross armband and small Red Cross sewn into the wing of his tunic collar. He carried his flat brief-case in a most business-like manner.

The German interrogator stood up and saluted and, followed by Beppo, made his exit.

Having shaken hands with me cordially, the Red Cross man clicked open the lid of his brief-case. Without looking at me he began:

"Now you understand, Sergeant, I have not much time. I have also other camps to visit. You are well-treated here? Enough food, for example?"

"No complaints about the food," I told him.

"That is good. Then all you have to do is to complete the Red Cross form.'

He slid the paper across the desk. It was headed "THE INTER-NATIONAL RED CROSS SOCIETY — PRISONERS-OF-WAR REGISTRATION FORM."

Then fixing me with his piercing grey eyes, he handed me a fountain-pen.

I wrote my R.A.F. number, my rank, my surname and my Christian names in the spaces provided. Then I replaced the cap on his pen, reached across the desk and put it down on the blotter in front of him.

"No, Sergeant, you must answer all the questions. Then will the Red Cross be able to notify your people that you are a prisoner-of-war."

"I'm sure they only need to know my number, rank and name," I objected, glancing down at the remaining questions:

Age:

Home Address:

Date of joining the Services:

Unit:

Where were you based?:

How long have you served abroad?:

By what means did you travel from your native country?:

There were other such questions and, at the bottom, space for a signature. The Red Cross Officer barked:

"Until you are a registered prisoner-of-war you have no protection at all! You understand, Sergeant? — No protection, no rights!"

I understood only too well.

"You are German?" I asked politely.

"Swiss!" he snapped, then, controlling his anger, added with honeydew concern, "Also will your family receive no news. You will be missing, believed killed!"

I said nothing but inwardly I was seething.

He glanced at my wedding-ring. "Your wife will much suffer. They will tell her she is a widow."

I glimpsed Beppo outside removing the door-key of that little building.

"You understand the Red Cross are neutral, so whatever you write on this paper is private." He was again offering me his pen.

I looked at him in disbelief and shook my head. He stood up.

"Very well! If you will not help the Red Cross, the Red Cross will not help you!"

Beppo was out of sight now and the early swifts were swooping above the wall. Fancy returning from England to such an unlovely place as this!

"Think about it, Sergeant. You are not protected by the Geneva Convention. No-one may ever know what happens to you." His tone was threatening.

He watched me closely as I gazed out of the window at the concrete hut. And praying for protection, I knew in that eternity that the companion I'd chummed up with in the desert was still close beside me.

"At least you will sign the form?"

I took the pen and printed my name.

His consequent anger surprised me. Gone was the suave Red Cross officer. He towered over me. He thumped Beppo's desk. He shrieked and shouted and threatened. I couldn't understand what I had said or done so to offend the Red Cross.

46

CHAPTER 7   RED DOUBLE-CROSS

Finally he replaced the form in his brief-case and, without another word, stalked out of the office.

Alberto looked positively distressed as he escorted me back to the compound.

Returning to the tent, I found Johnny angrily pointing at the corner where I'd left my newly-acquired water-bottle. I gathered that Sloucher had removed it during my absence.

Sometime in the late afternoon, while we were strolling round the compound, Sloucher led in a jaunty KD-clad POW.

We hastened to welcome him.

"Gee, am I glad to meet someone who speaks English!" he drawled.

I explained that, although Johnny had no English, he was a good friend.

"I'm RCAF, air-gunner on Baltimores, Sam's the name, shot down near Bardia. I didn't know they had any fighters left, but this bastard appeared from nowhere and filled us with holes. A Junkers 88, of course."

He'd given all this information even before we reached the tent!

As soon as Sloucher had departed, I put my finger to my lips and halted Sam in full flow. He looked puzzled.

Then, his face brightening, "Sure! Careless talk and all that jazz! Sorry!" He paused to grin at the Gurkha before adding, "I'd rather yammer about dames anyway."

And yammer about dames he did — all through the macaroni supper, late into the night and during the greater part of the following morning. Understanding absolutely nothing Johnny smiled politely from time to time, invariably in the wrong places. As for me I couldn't have cared less about the Canadian chicks, for then, more than ever, my heart was weeping for my love.

When at last he broke off suddenly, it was to point towards the gate.

"Look, Ken, they're bringing in another POW!"

I looked. I could scarce contain my delight. The newcomer, wearing RAF battledress top complete with pilot's wings, was none other than my skipper and good friend, Hal!

I hurried out of the tent to meet him. When he saw me his eyes momentarily lit up with pleasure, but then he deliberately turned his head away. We exchanged greetings as though we had never seen each other before, careful to give no indication, either to friend or foe, that we belonged to the same aircrew.

Later, walking in the compound, he told me his story.

Alone in the aircraft after we had baled out, he too had reached for his parachute. And in that fearful moment he knew that he could never bale out. As a result of his exertions in correcting the yaw of the failing port engine, his foot had jammed in the rudder-bar.

By that time the Wellington was losing height at an alarming rate. She shuddered slightly as he yanked hard back on the stick. Suddenly rising out of the shadows ahead was the hump of a hill. Nothing Hal could do but brace himself and pray. And by a miracle against all the laws of aerodynamics, the Wellington spirited itself over the crest.

Whereupon he saw a wide valley rushing up to meet him. A last desperate heave on the stick. The breathless wait for oblivion. But oblivion did not come. The miracle was still happening for in that jot of time she lifted her nose. Then, her undercart still retracted, she slithered across the flat ground, splintering her belly, finally coming to rest in a hummock of dust . . .

Hal stopped and rubbed his forehead just above the left eye.

"See the bruise. It's where I cracked my head on the instrument panel. Knocked me out for a few seconds. When I came to I shut off the petrol-cocks, climbed out and got away as quick as I could. Luckily she didn't catch fire. As soon as it was safe I went back to her. She was canted over onto her port wing, both props buckled." . . .

Supporting himself against the bulkhead he made his way towards the navigation table. Then he reached up for the Verey pistol and loaded it with the first cartridge that came to hand. He pushed open the astrodome, raised the pistol to the vertical and fired. The sky was lit with two streaks of bright red which finally died away in feathery smoke.

Then he did exactly as I had done. One by one he cried out the names of our crew, listening first to the silence and then to the faraway echoes.

A few minutes later he fired another cartridge, red-green this time. Again he called for us; again there was no reply.

So he did until all of eight cartridges had flared and perished; until he was hoarse from shouting.

Next he picked up his Air-Force-blue webbing satchel and methodically packed it with essential items. In all he did Hal was methodical. The First-Aid kit; a full water-bottle and a couple of flasks he filled from the aircraft water-supply; the Mercator's chart which bore my navigation plot; a tin of tomato juice, and, what was always essential to Hal, his cigarettes and matches — these were the final contents of his neatly-packed satchel.

He scrambled out of the cockpit for the last time, cast one regretful look at Wellington B-for Bertie and set off walking in a north-easterly direction.

The time by his gold watch was half-past one in the morning . . .

At this point Hal paused, for Sam was striding along behind us. He added, "Strange you didn't see the flares, Ken!" and I had time to reply, "We were probably miles apart. I didn't even hear anything."

Then Sam caught up with us, clapping us both on our shoulders.

"Hey fellers, mind if I join you?"

"Sure!" I said and, in order to keep him off the subject of women, informed him, "Hal here tells me he did his training in Canada."

Thereupon Hal asked Sam if he knew the Flying Training School at Medicine Hat and they started chatting.

I remained silent, dropping behind a little and noting the contrast between them. Both were fair but Sam's hair was sleek, Hal's thin and slightly curly; Sam's complexion smooth, Hal's ruddy and weatherbeaten; Sam clean-

48

shaven, Hal moustached with the first sprouting of a beard; Sam boyish, Hal mature and self-assured.

Yet I was quickly to discover that Sam's flippancy was only a mask. As we reached the tent he turned to me abruptly and demanded:

"Say Ken, whatever happened to your knees?"

"I scraped them on the shingle," I told him. He stooped to make a closer examination, his manner assured and professional.

"How often have you bathed them?"

"Just once since I've been here. Before that I had no water."

He shook his head and tutted.

"This goddam filthy desert! "he grumbled. "The least scratch goes septic:"

"I've got some boracic and cotton-wool in my satchel," volunteered Hal.

"Okay then. Now all we need is hot water." Sam glanced significantly at Sloucher who had propped his rifle against the wire and was leaning against the gatepost picking his nose.

While Hal sorted the medical kit, Sam took my Mersa-Matruh messtin and hurried across to the compound gate. I followed, exaggerating my limp. By the time I arrived the comedy had begun. Sam, making liquid noises, was dipping his finger into the tin and withdrawing it sharply as if scalded.

"Hot water!" he explained to Sloucher at the end of the performance, and at the top of his Canadian voice, "We — want — hot — water."

Sloucher stopped his nose-picking, took up his rifle. and scowled.

"Hot water, you cloth-eared clot" Sloucher clicked off the safety-catch.

Luckily Alberto appeared at that moment, coming to relieve his mate.

"Per favore — acqua calda!" I translated.

Alberto beamed at us, hurried forward to the gate and accepted the messtin through a gap between the barbed-wire strands.

"Subito!" he replied. Then with a terse "Momento!" to Sloucher he was on his way back to the guard-room.

To our relief the safety-catch was clicked forward and in a couple of minutes Alberto returned.

"Mille grazie!" I thanked him as he handed back the steaming tin.

"Prego!" he reiterated. Then smartly he took up his post outside the gate while Sloucher grumbled a few words and stumped away.

It wasn't until the knee-bathing was completed and the boracic applied that Sam remarked:

"I didn't know you spoke the lingo, Ken."

"Only a few words. Come to that I didn't know you were a first-aider."

"Sure! I'm aiming to go in for medicine. The old man's a quack back home."

At that moment the lunch arrived and I made haste to wash out my messtin.

Afterwards Alberto came to take Johnny Gurkha from us. I was sad at being parted from such a cheerful companion but we smiled at each other and shook hands warmly. I watched his lithe figure until it was out of sight behind the camp buildings.

When I returned to the tent Hal was asleep, and I realised then how tired he must have been.

Thus it was not until late afternoon that I heard the rest of his story.

He had walked until early morning of this, the ninth day. From the start he had taken frequent rests and resisted the temptation to hurry. He had travelled at night and also during the early and late part of the day. When there were no stars to see he used his watch for direction, aligning the hour hand with the sun and bisecting the angle subtended with the minute hand, to find the North-South line.

At about four o' clock in the morning he had come to a broad track running north-south. A truck was approaching from the south. To his delight he recognised it as a British gharry. He stepped into the middle of the track and hailed it, frantically waving his arms.

The gharry stopped, but his delight turned to despair when he saw that the occupants were German!

They gave him a lift all right! Directly to Mersa Matruh! . . .

The next morning Hal was required for further questioning. This as he told me later, was in three parts; a preliminary bout with the comic-opera commandant; a round of canny sparring with the German Intelligence officer, and the entertainment closed with the ploy of Red Cross officer with Red Cross form.

He returned in his KD outfit highly indignant.

"The blighters have pinched my battledress top and the first-aid kit!" he announced.

"What about the Mercator's chart?" I asked.

Hal looked even more hurt.

"Ken, you know me better than that! I got rid of it when we stopped at a fuel depot on the way. They let me use the latrines, you see. All the pieces are well covered by squares of German newspaper. I shouldn't think anybody would want to fish it out and fit it together."

"Good work, Hal!" laughed Sam, adding, "But how come they took your battledress? Did they rip it off you or something?"

"They told me they were taking it for safekeeping."

"Thieving bastards!" snorted Sam . . .

The following day brought one more prisoner — a pale bespectacled man with a Putney accent. He spoke nostalgically of football at Fulham, tennis at Wimbledon and jellied eels at Walham Green. He said he was in an armoured-car which had been hit by a Panzer-shell. He'd been blown out of the turret before it went up in flames.

He was intensely serious and suspiciously voluble. We were even more suspicious when he began asking questions.

His accent, certainly, was genuine south-west London, but he lacked the essential English quality — a sense of humour.

CHAPTER 7   RED DOUBLE-CROSS

He called himself George and told us he was with the Long Range Desert Group.

"Never heard of them!" pretended Hal.

"We reconnoitre behind enemy lines," retorted George, "I'm surprised you have not heard tell of us!"

"I guess it's been kept a secret," Sam remarked, feigning admiration, "Gee, you boys must have had some experiences!"

"No more than you chaps, I expect. Were you with a Canadian Squadron"

"Hand-picked maple-leaf aces, all of us!" came the drawled reply.

George's irritation was ill-concealed. He turned to Hal.

"What type of aircraft were you flying, Sergeant?"

"Ox-boxes!" Hal informed him gravely. We rejoiced in the bewilderment of George, who was nothing more or less than a German "plant."

"Don't you know what 'ox-boxes' are?" I exclaimed and Sam added that he guessed everybody knew that.

"Airspeed Oxfords," explained Hal, "carrying torpedoes, you know."

George gave him a murderous look. Of course he knew that Oxfords were twin-engined trainers. He knew also that we would all three have heard of the Long Range Desert Group. Furthermore he knew that he had failed in his mission.

Half an hour later a smiling Alberto removed him from our presence . . .

Later in the day a batch of twenty POW's were brought in — a mixture of Geordies, Scouses and Cockneys. Two of them, Durham Light Infantrymen, had terrible leg-wounds and hobbled along, supported by their mates.

That night was disturbed by their groans and the occasional cries of a soldier whose nerves had been shattered in the nightmare of battle.

In the morning, immediately after we had breakfasted, a large open truck rumbled into the camp and halted near the compound entrance.

Amid a raucous shouting of orders, four Schmeisser-armed Germans dismounted from the back and an officer from the cab. The driver remained at the wheel. Beppo appeared carrying a piece of paper. While the German officer was signing this, Sloucher was unlocking the gate.

"Raus! Raus!" yelled the guards, spurring our unceremonious departure.

They shoved us forward, well and wounded alike and within a couple of minutes we were sitting on the metal floor of the truck, the tail-board closed up and a guard at each corner.

With our backs to the cab, Hal and I watched the compound, the Commandant's office and the small white building beginning jerkily to move away. When we reached the main gate Hal suddenly leant forward and pointed.

"Ken look! There's that German stooge. He's wearing my battledress!"

George was standing in front of the guard-tent. As our truck roared past him he glanced down at his newly-won pilot's wings. Then he favoured us with a triumphant grin . . .

CHAPTER 8

Tobruk again

Mercifully during the greater part of the journey the nerve-shattered DLI slept the sleep of exhaustion. The injuries of his two mates were pitiful — torn flesh, yellow with pus, exposed to infection from flies swarming in the heat and from dust rising out of sand-swathes on the macadam road. Neither of the men seemed to have the strength nor the will to brush the flies away.

"I'm gonna clean up those guys!" muttered Sam and, water-bottle in hand, began to make his way across the truck. He was stopped in his tracks by an angry shout and the click of an automatic rifle. The guard nearest us was taking aim! Sam squatted down where he was and, at the top of his voice, began a tale about a red-head he'd known in Montreal . . .

Mersa Matruh was soon lost to view. The road climbed up onto the desert plateau and there aligned itself once more with the coast.

Near Sidi Barrani the driver stopped at a refuelling depot. We were allowed down from the truck to drink from a stand-pipe. The warm liquid was slightly saline but it helped to relieve our thirst and those few POWs with water-bottles were able to fill them.

Immediately we had helped the injured men on board again Sam bathed their wounds with Sidi Barrani water and bandaged them with strips torn from their KD shirts.

Hal manufactured a cigarette from his tin of dogends, and I was surprised to see him produce a tiny box of matches.

"They were lying on the Commandant's desk!" he chuckled, "While they were examining my battledress, I hid them on my person!"

After lighting up his cigarette he took an envelope from his satchel and handed it to me, saying, "Did I ever show you these photos, Ken?"

I shook my head. I had only ever seen one photo of his family — the framed enlargement that he'd kept on his locker, back at O.T.U. Harwell.

One by one I took these snaps out of the envelope; his wife Vi, blonde and slim, with laughter in her eyes, cradling baby Rodney in her arms; Vi on her own; Rodney's four-year-old sister, Janice, clutching her doll; and one of Hal and Vi with Janice when she was a baby.

Hal sighed deeply as I returned the envelope.

"That's the worst part — our families being told we're missing. Then they make our wives fill in Widows' Pension Forms. That's why we've damn well got to escape!"

"It's hell for the wives," I agreed, "just waiting, not knowing whether we're alive or dead — that's torture!" I glanced at the guards. "But it would be suicide to try to get away now."

Hal nodded.

"We'll bide our time," he murmured.

The truck lumbered, groaning, through Halfaya Pass and up over the shoulder of the hill. Longtime we looked down upon Sollum's tranquil bay. Followed the last hour of our wearisome journey before we jolted to a halt in the wrecked seaside village of Bardia.

Within an oblong of barbed wire half-a-dozen Italian-style tents awaited us. These were constructed of groundsheets buttoned together over an oblong frame. The sheets could also be used as capes. It really was a brilliant idea for dry-weather camping, but somewhat inconvenient when it rained as the water then jetted through the buttonholes!

However that night was dry. There must have been some dampness at the foot of the hill for several thousand bull-frogs were rasping in chorus.

Bull-frogs or no bull-frogs, most of us were so exhausted that we lay down and fell asleep immediately. As Sam informed us the following morning, even the wounded slept . . .

We were roused soon after sunrise and herded back into the truck.

This day's journey westward was as tiring as the previous one. The sun was as hot, the flies as numerous, our thirst as torturesome. But from time to time we threaded valleys green with palm and broom, and shining with flowers — moments of delight after so many months in the dead wasteland.

Sam's ministrations had done much to comfort the wounded, and, reaching Gambut after about two hours' chugging, we were actually given some food. They were tins of meat; and, although it was not politic to enquire whether the meat was primarily intended for humans or animals, it was sustenance when swilled down with Gambut water. Our morale improved considerably.

As we continued, I wondered if we should see something of the damage our bombs had caused in Tobruk. It had been our target night after night — so much so that we called it "The mail run!" We felt that we had gone a long way towards achieving our objective of destroying harbour installations, fuel storages and shipping.

"It must be a shambles down there!" I remarked and Hal nodded.

A tall thin POW leaned across to us. When he pointed towards the high ground away to the left, I noticed Sergeant's stripes on his tattered shirtsleeve.

"It's over there, see — El Adem. That's where the Indians put up a hell of a good fight back in June. We were up Gazala way waiting our turn . . ."

"Bloody murder it was!" exclaimed one of the wounded men, sitting up suddenly. Then as he winced with pain from his lacerated thigh, we heard him mutter, "We was boxed in see."

The Sergeant stroked his stubbly chin reflectively.

"Funny how it all works out," he said, "Bert here, he comes all through that Tobruk affair without a scratch, then cops this shrapnel from a stray shell at Alamein. We'd just been saying how quiet it was!"

54

CHAPTER 8   TOBRUK AGAIN

"Whatever happened to this guy?" asked Sam, gently bathing the other man's leg below the knee.

"Jack was out on patrol. His mate set off a mine!" replied the Sergeant.

There was a long pause in the conversation while the truck dropped noisily into low gear and we entered the outskirts of Tobruk. We were amazed that so many buildings were still intact. Nevertheless destruction was extensive round the harbour. We glimpsed one ship damaged beyond repair and we could only guess at the number of wrecks lying beneath the surface. The quayside was littered with piles of rubble, charred timbers and chunks of grotesquely twisted metal.

Tobruk is only a small harbour but for Rommel it was the only possible harbour. Because it was small, its defenders could treat each attacking Allied bomber to a vicious concentration of flak. In those days each bomber crew acted independently, although fulfilling briefing instructions as to the direction and approximate time of attack. Aircraft therefore tended to attack, one after the other, in much the same order as they had taken off from Base. However, as the time margin was small and as different navigators used slightly different routes, it also often happened that two or three aircraft went in simultaneously, thus sharing the warmth of the enemy's reception. On the other hand, the searchlights and guns could be so busy with one aircraft that they were sometimes slow to pick up the arrival of the next.

Making a bombing run at 6000 feet over Tobruk, the only aircraft in the sky, was a terrifying experience.

"Ken, remember our quiet night?" asked Hal as the truck began to climb out of the town.

I laughed. It was the night of 4th/5th August when we'd been briefed to stay over the target for an hour, cruising to and fro to keep the guns busy. The theory was that, while the gunners were firing at us, they wouldn't notice that the Royal Navy were sailing in from the north nor that the British Army were moving up from the south.

We should not have been flying at all that night. We'd done an eight-hour trip on the 3rd August and, as we were officially "on rest" that afternoon, we had been asked to take some people up to Palestine. In front of the mess at Aqir aerodrome was a pleasant garden, and the paths were bounded by concrete snaketrap ditches.

That hour of relaxation at Aqir was a little bit of Heaven.

We landed back at base to find turmoil everywhere. The "reserve aircraft" we were flying was required for ops that night and we were the crew detailed to fly it. It seemed the army and navy were going to re-capture Tobruk in the small hours of the morning and it was our task to provide a diversion.

Of course, there had been a security leak in Cairo and some Arab had sold the information to the enemy. Tobruk's guns were trained seawards and we cruised about with greater safety than if we had been in a trainer over the Liverpool estuary where the Merchant Navy did occasionally poop off at us!

ESCAPE FROM ASCOLI

For us the dramatic moment didn't arrive until we had taxied to the dispersal strip at Base after nearly nine hours in the air. Our ground crew, who had come to meet us, suddenly turned tail and ran away. Then one mechanic tiptoed stealthily back carrying a large spanner.

We clambered out of the Wellington to find him holding up the limp body of a brightly-coloured Palestinian viper!

It was too dry for snakes at Base. The viper had been sleeping in the cubby-hole where the wheels retracted. He'd had ten hours' flying, including an hour over Tobruk, covering in all some 1300 miles.

CHAPTER 9

Flies undone!

Now our truck was taking us across the hillside where the Germans used to switch on dummy fires in order to confuse us navigators. Hal was not smiling now. He was looking back for the last time at that all-too-familiar harbour. I knew precisely what he was thinking and my laughter also died.

In that moment our hearts were sad for good friends who had perished there . . .

It was mid-afternoon when we paused briefly on the Gazala cliffs. There was little to see as the wind was whipping up a dust-storm.

"It was mostly always like this in May," remarked the Sergeant.

"Except that it was hotter!" observed Bert as Sam helped him to his feet.

"Like a bloody furnace!" exclaimed Jack, struggling to get up unassisted. In the end it needed three of us to lift him down from the lorry. Then, clutching the sergeant's arm, he hobbled about as if he were on hallowed ground, telling Sam that in this place he'd watched Hurricanes shooting down Stukas one after another.

I reflected that, since being captured, the only enemy aircraft I'd seen in the sky were two Junkers 88s and two Junkers 52s.

"Reckon they're running short of fuel," Hal commented . . .

We weren't sorry to be ordered back into the truck to get away from that inhospitable plateau. Longtime the blown sand remained in our ears, eyes, teeth and nostrils.

The road branched northwest parallel to the coastline and over the fringe of the Akdar hills. Then for several miles it led us through a succession of green ravines, finally descending steeply about a thousand feet into the lovely seaside village of Derna. Here the air was fragrant with the scents of many flowers; and gardens, set in marble courts, were rich with vines and other fruits. We saw figs and pomegranates and bananas as our prison-truck made for another rectangle of barbed wire wherein yet another formation of Italian-style tents were waiting to receive us.

We were put in the charge of a posse of surly-looking Fascist guards while the Germans went off to relax in the village.

There were a dozen tents in all so that when we were accommodated four men to a tent, six still remained empty. As at Mersa we were expected to sleep on the bare ground — even the wounded.

Accordingly, as soon as I thought the Fascists were outside the wire, I sauntered along to the nearest empty tent and began undoing its buttons.

The groundsheets of which it was composed would help Bert and his mate Jack through the night.

I'd not succeeded in opening even one set of flies before I received a sickening thump on the back of my head. My forehead struck a tent-frame to which I clung tightly to prevent myself from falling. The other tents seemed to be jigging about in the evening sky, and a falsetto voice was screaming at me in fury.

When things steadied down a bit I stood up and faced my assailant. He was a stocky, snarling gentleman with stripes on his arm.

I tried to tell him that I was only borrowing the groundsheets.

"Rimette! Rimette!" he screamed, gesticulating wildly.

I tried to explain once more. He replied by jerking out his revolver.

I did my utmost to tell him that I wanted the groundsheets for the wounded and that I was a sergeant.

"Io sergente-maggiore!" His eyes bulged as he took aim, releasing the safety-catch.

Without further ado I re-fastened the buttons, wondering whether I would actually hear the shot if he pressed the trigger.

When I turned round he was striding towards the gate, revolver in holster . . .

"You're an idiot!" scolded Hal, "From now on suicidal risks are out. When we escape every risk will be calculated." He stubbed out his dog-end and replaced it in a near-empty tin. Then he lay back staring up at the tent's flat camouflaged roof. Opposite us Sam and Bert were conversing in low tones.

"Fifteen days ago at this time, Ken, we were just taking off."

"Only fifteen days!" I echoed, "it seems a lifetime!"

"I don't suppose our wives even know we're missing. They'll probably still be receiving our letters."

Just seventeen days ago, in the cool comfort of the New Zealand Club in Cairo, I'd written Lillian an airgraph letter. So many things I was not allowed to say that it amounted to no more than describing my ride on a camel, how colour can still be seen on the Pyramids' inner walls and how the Sphinx lost its nose to a Napoleonic cannonball. It was meant to amuse and to cheer her. Yet above all it was meant to tell her how sorely I missed her, how achingly I loved her.

When I turned to speak to Hal again he was fast asleep. I looked across at Sam who put his finger to his lips because Bert also was sleeping. Then he too closed his eyes.

Through the tent opening I could discern the eye of the moon, closed except for a delicate arc of light.

The night was quiet but not silent like a desert night. The calling of owls and the occasional bleating of sheep mingled with the subdued voices of fellow-prisoners in the other tents. But beyond those sounds, from the direction of the village itself, I distinguished music from a radio — the

CHAPTER 9   FLIES UNDONE!

German soldiers' song which so aptly expressed my feelings "LILLI MAR-LENE!"

"I knew you were waiting there for me . . .
You'd always be
My Lily of the lamp-light,
My own Lilli Marlene!"
That summed it up:

Waiting — that's what the war meant to people like us. Waiting for an end to the torture of separation, waiting for home to be truly home again, not just a place for weekend leave whenever we could both get it.

"Darling, to be parted was more than I could bear!"

We had kissed goodbye near Harwell aerodrome whence, via Cornwall and Gibraltar, I'd come to North Africa . . .

Sleep, when it came, was sweet oblivion . . .

The German guards returned to us in good mood next morning. They gave us time for a last drink of the delicious Derna water and for Sam to finish bathing and re-bandaging the wounded. I took my chance and cadged a cigarette for Hal from one of them. He was the one who, presently, with a nod and a grin, indicated that we should get aboard.

Growling reluctantly, the truck inched its way up the hill between steep green flower-decked slopes at the top of which we turned westwards yet again. There was a redness in the soil which gradually faded as we distanced ourselves from Derna.

The road skirted the northern foothills of the Akdar mountains, for a long time hugging the coast so that we were able to gaze down upon the tranquillity of the Med. After an hour it swung away inland, but the wilderness through which we passed was punctuated by green ravines and precipitous gradients. Because of the surrounding hills there were no far horizons as in the desert.

At midday we paused near Barche to refuel. The water here was not as sweet as the water of Derna nor as saline and brackish as the water of the Western Desert. By now we were all hungry for, apart from half a tin of questionable meat, we had had nothing to eat since leaving Mersa Matruh. The guards, munching bread and meat, informed us that we would soon be in the POW Camp at Benghazi.

"They will feed you there!" said the guard who had given me a cigarette. When I thanked him for the information, he threw me another.

Hal did not light it until we were on our way. Over near the coast salt flats began to appear, brilliant in the afternoon sun; while to the south were stretches of red sand. We saw isolated clusters of date palms as we came down onto an open plain, the cliffs flattening out to reveal the harbour of Benghazi.

"It's not such a big harbour after all," commented Hal.

However there was a fair-sized ship at the quayside and another anchored out in the bay.

Now the POW Camp was ahead of us. We distinguished two or three barbed-wire compounds. I moved close to Hal.

"What are the chances of meeting up with our crew?" I asked quietly.

"Quite good, I should think. If they'd walked north to give themselves up near Mersa, they'd have been captured a week before us. At that rate they could have left the interrogation camp before you got there, Ken."

We were greatly cheered at the possibility of a re-union with Bert and Alf and Taffy and Bryn. However, as we drew nearer, we could see that the compounds were crammed with thousands of POWs.

"Hal, if they are there, we'll have some job in finding them."

He nodded, adding, "unless they see us arrive, of course."

The big barbed-wire gate swung open as we drew to a halt.

"Raus! Raus!" shouted the guards fiercely and we scrambled down from the truck.

As at Derna we were handed over to the custody of the Fascists. Here however we were lined up and searched. The search was hasty and not too thorough. A caporale admired my comb-case and returned it to me, complete with escape-saw!

We too were searching, scrutinising the sea of faces in the compounds on either side of us. Whenever a fresh batch of POWs was brought in, hundreds would come to stand and watch. Many, like us, were seeking missing comrades, some were hoping to hear up-to-date news from those recently captured, some were there out of idle curiosity. Those in front were always in danger of being pushed against the trip-wire, an eventuality that could prove fatal.

Sentries had strict orders to shoot any POW who touched the trip-wire, a knee-high barbed-wire strand a few feet inside the fence. They shot to kill!

We looked in vain. There were many Australians and New Zealanders, but no Bert; many Cockneys, but no Alf; some Welsh but certainly not our Taffy Coles. Amongst the Indians we didn't need to search, only surprised at the huge number of them.

The sun was crimsoning the derricks and the superstructure of the ships over in the harbour when the inner gate was opened to us.

An RAMC sergeant greeted us with "Bring those wounded chaps along to the Medic's tent."

Sam and the sergeant complied while the rest of us were led in, besieged with questions, by the unofficial welcoming committee.

CHAPTER 10

Hell-ship

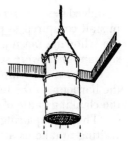

The gates closed and the Benghazi POWs began firing questions at us:
"Where was you captured, mate?"
"Have they stopped Jerry?"
"They still blitzing London?"
"What's rationing like in Blighty?"
Before any of us had time to reply, there sounded a tremendous thump. Then more thumps evenly spaced out. Finally a shattering explosion.

All voices hushed, all faces turned towards the harbour. Behind the huddled date-palms, slowly reaching skywards rose a pillar of black smoke. Around the tongue of flame at its base tiny figures were scurrying, obviously frantic to extinguish the fire before it reached the vital parts of their ship.

With one accord we found our voices, bursting forth in a prolonged cheer. A hollow-cheeked man in a tank-beret clutched my arm, pointed above his head and yelled in my ear:

"Look! There he is!"

Then everyone was looking up at the sky, silent again and listening. We watched that tiny point of light, we strained our ears to catch the faint rhythmic drone of the aircraft engine or engines. Our throbbing star moved away over the sea, finally disappearing behind glowing ribbons of cloud.

By this time the deck-fire had been put out and the smoke-pillar was no more than a grey shapeless smudge above the quay. Although this raid by a lone bomber had caused very little damage to the enemy, to us it was a great morale-booster. We decided that there might be an aircraft-carrier steaming not too far off the coast.

Hal and I searched the camp for the rest of our crew. But all in vain. No sign anywhere of Bert or Taffy or Bryn or Alf. Indeed of the very few RAF POWs at Benghazi at that time, all had been captured long since and none could give us any news.

Sam had become a medical orderly at the "hospital tents" where we also saw our wounded travelling-companions. Jack winked and gave us a thumbs-up sign, nodding towards Bert who was sleeping.

Finally we fitted ourselves into a tiny space just inside one of the tents farthest from the open latrine-pits.

From his webbing-satchel Hal took out his old exercise-book and pencil. Looking over his shoulder I saw him write:

6th October, 1942 — Arrived BENGHAZI. The whole place stinks.

61

Indeed heat, overcrowding, inadequate washing facilities and open latrine-pits all conspired to produce the omnipresent stench. When the sun got up the following morning so did the flies, swarms of them. Small wonder that so many men were suffering from dysentery.

The hoot of a ship's siren was the prelude to a burst of activity down at the harbour — the to-ing and fro-ing of trucks, the whirring of machinery, the clanking rattle of a crane.

"They're repairing the bomb damage," declared Hal, "Maybe that ship's waiting to take us across to Italy."

"Sometimes they use Junkers 52s," I said wistfully, remembering how some POWs had overpowered their guards and flown a Ju 52 back to Allied territory.

"One thing's certain, Ken. We've no chance of escaping from this filthy hole." . . .

Four days later in the food-queue we were greeted by the taller of the two Australians who occupied the tent next to ours.

"Hey Pommies, did you know there's a batch off to Italy tomorrow?"

When we showed surprise, he continued:

"Cobber an' me's goin . . ."

"Or supposed to be!" put in Cobber, adding confidentially, "I'll tell you straight — we want out! The last shipload was torpedoed. Gotter tell you that to be fair, see."

We moved forward to collect our chippaties upon which we balanced our small white lumps of ghi.

As we made our way back the taller Aussie explained:

"It's got round that you two jokers aren't all that keen on stayin' here. Well you can have our berths if you're that dead-set. No names was taken."

"We won't think badly of you if you say 'No'," said Cobber, "Most o' the fellers 'ud give their right arms to stay here anyway . . ."

"Stay in this stinking hole!" exclaimed Hal, "Not us!"

"We'll swop places with you," I agreed, "But don't think we're heroes. It's just that whatever we do is a risk. Here we risk dysentery and the plagues of Africa. We'd rather chance the torpedoes."

The Aussies looked immensely relieved.

"Gotter be at the main gate first thing in the morning," Cobber informed us, trying to hide his exultation.

Then the pair vanished into their tent. We never saw them again . . .

Next day soon after sunrise we were among the crowd squatting on the red-streaked sand near the main gate.

Trucks coming up from the south brought in this red dust on their tyre-treads. I was fascinated by this geometrical pattern of four sharply delineated colours: Martian-red down towards the desert; pallid-white stretching from the camp to the town; a silver brilliance that denoted the salt flats and almost at the same level, the turquoise sea.

"Wakey-wakey, Ken! The Eyeties want us to line up!"

CHAPTER 10   HELL-SHIP

I scrambled to my feet as the Fascist guards set about arranging us in lines of four. It was a pantomine of gesticulation and shouting, with the POWs purposely obtuse.

"Aspetti qui! . . . Là, là, là . . . Guiseppe, quanto prigioneri lì? . . . Dov'è il caporale? . . . Si, sì! dai capelli rossi!"

This was followed by the ever-hilarous comedy of counting.

"Quarantasette, quarant'otto, quarantanove!" Fortynine! But there should be fifty in each group!

The soldato semplice waited for his companion who was walking down the opposite flank also counting:

"Quarant'otto, quarantanove! . . . Si, sì! Soltanto quarantanove!"

They returned to the front and started again, failing to observe a guardsman surreptitiously joining us from the group behind.

The soldato semplice arrived on the left flank at the rear, smiling:

"Quarantanove — cinquanta . . . Ecco!"

His comrade on the right now came abreast of us:

"Quarantanove — cinquanta — cinquant'uno! . . . Perchè?!"

We knew why there were now fifty-one. The red-haired corporal who had been sitting down hidden by his mates, had decided to stand up!

Such diversions relieved the monotony of the long wait. We stood around there during the whole of the morning, received our chippaties and ghi at midday, and then waited during the early part of the afternoon.

At long last, at exactly four o'clock by Hal's watch, we were lined up and counted again. Then the gates were opened to allow us to amble out.

When the head of the column reached the cluster of date-palms, its tail was just outside the camp gates. I wondered how this huge crocodile of men could fit itself into just one boat. Maybe there were two boats?

We had several more halts before arriving at the quayside where we sat and waited again.

At six o'clock we began filing up the gang-plank, a lengthy procedure for several hundred men of several nations. I searched the sky for the moving speck that would betoken a recce plane but saw nothing but a stray wisp of cloud.

I tried to convince myself that a photo recce would have been carried out; that the Royal Navy, duly advised that this was a POW-transporter, would refrain from torpedoing it . . . Please God! . . .

The soles of my plimsolls were by now pitifully thin so that I found the uneven metal surfaces painful to tread on. Some of them were still surprisingly hot!

Two Fascist guards stood by the open hatch, impatiently urging us forward, menacing us with revolvers. The steady flow never faltered, the sick, wounded and half-starved moved into the hatch and down the steep companion at the pace of the rest.

Hal slung his satchel round his neck, letting it hang behind him as he descended, rung by rung, into the darkness of the hold. I followed close behind him, just keeping clear of the feet of the man coming after me.

When I got to the bottom Hal caught my arm and steadied me. I leant against a pillar, took a deep breath and looked around me. Only then did I comprehend the utter horror of the situation into which we had been cast.

The Indians had been packed in first and the place was filled with the babble of various languages. The gloom was the gloom of a Hell-hole even though the hatch was not yet battened down; and the smell, even at this early stage, was the smell of several hundred close-confined human bodies. And still the pitiful human cargo was pouring in down the companion!

In the middle of the hold stood two large open oil-drums. A pair of holes had been bored near the top of each to accommodate ropes suspended from pulleys near the hatch opening.

"Behold the mod cons!" said Hal as we took up residence on a few square feet of iron grating bordering a stanchion. Hal supported his back against this as he wrote in his book:

"12th October, 1942 Guests of Regia Marina."

No sooner had he finished writing when, with an outburst of shouting, the hatches were slammed shut. We could vaguely discern the shapes of men still coming down the companion. A thud and a cry denoted that someone had fallen. Whether he was helped away or whether he just lay there in agony, we were never to know. Such was the overcrowding that only those nearby would have been able to get to assist him.

We had descended into Hell, there was no doubt about that. Hell was a steel-plated dungeon seething with the damned, filled with groans and cries of sudden anguish and progressively stinking in the airless heat.

Gradually, with the reluctant light filtering through chinks in the deck plating, the first terrible darkness faded. The obscurity which replaced it was even more horrifying, for through it we were better able to witness the sufferings around us: the coughing and retching of the sick; the contortions of pain of the wounded; the skeletal weakness of the half-starved; the miserable procession of men staggering over the bodies of their comrades towards the latrine buckets.

Hal shook his head sadly, laid his head back on his satchel and closed his eyes. I doubt whether he slept. Maybe closing his eyes helped to shut out the horror of the place. For me that horror could never be shut out nor ever in my life forgotten.

The Twelfth of October, 1942! Hal's neat writing was still clear in my mind. I remembered that on this very day 150 years ago, Cristofero Colomb of Genoa reached the shores of San Salvador. On the "Santa Maria" verminous food, shortage of drinking water and terror of the unknown had been for his crew the ingredients of a Little Hell. But at least the sea and the sky had been theirs to behold, the clean air theirs to breathe. Nor was their little ship as overloaded as ours must have been.

CHAPTER 10 HELL-SHIP

When I, too, closed my eyes, I felt as strongly as in the desert the presence of an unseen companion whose voice was clear above the babble around me.

"Endure and have faith."

Came the first strokes of the ship's engine, hammering through my consciousness like crucifixion nails. Up there in the World of Light, the siren uttered a shrill screech; and our steel-plated cage shuddered as the hell-ship began to move.

To the clanking rhythm of the pistons the couplet from *"Paradise Lost" drummed over and over in my mind:

"The mind is its own place, and in itself,

Can make a Heav'n of Hell, a Hell of Heav'n."

They were the words of Satan! . . .

Suddenly an idea dawned in my mind:

"Hal, there could be a chance of being intercepted by the Royal Navy!"

Hal opened his eyes wearily, not really listening.

"A couple of destroyers say! They could rescue us!"

For reply he only sighed, shook his head hopelessly and once again closed his eyes . . .

We would be steaming north, I reckoned, probably making for Taranto in the arch of Italy's foot or Brindisi in its heel. I didn't think they'd take us to Sicily or through the Messina Straits.

The Pole Star would be ahead and the moon a finely-traced curve just entering its first quarter. The sky would be cloudless as all the nights had been, and we would be grinding on at the rate of some 12 knots. Fortunately the sea was calm. I shuddered at the possibility of a storm blowing up because we must have been seriously overloaded. The loading-line would be well-submerged, and down in the hold we would be below the surface of the water.

For us a heavy storm was almost as much to be dreaded as an accurate torpedo . . .

I lay motionless, eyes tight-shut, and prayed. Whenever, as frequently happened, people stumbled over me, I said nothing, remaining completely inert.

With the deepening darkness, the stench from the already overflowing latrine-drums became ever more nauseating; and, because of the fearful overcrowding, every drawn breath was an effort.

I made myself think of lovely Dorset, its heath and hills and woods and bays; of my love and I exploring them together . . .

When at last I opened my eyes again, the morning light was showing above us at the edges of the steel plates in thinly-ruled rectangles. Footsteps clanged on the deck. Came a shouted command, a violent clatter of bolts and we were dazzled by a sudden blaze as the hatches were thrown open.

Two POWs were ordered out to haul up the latrine-drums. Just as they

* "Paradise Lost" Book I — 1.254–5 — John Milton.

heaved on the ropes the ship began to roll. The first of the drums rose jerkily, swaying and circling and spilling. Finally it was man-handled through the open hatch and we heard it being dragged across the deck to be emptied and hosed.

Then the second drum was lifted out and emptied in the same way.

Finally the drums were lowered again and placed in position. The degradation, whereby human beings were treated worse than cattle, was to continue throughout the fetid heat of the day.

Once again the hatches were shut and bolted; and as the sun burned down outside, our steel cage became an airless oven.

Before the torture of that day was over, life had become almost insupportable. Morale was at its lowest ebb: death or continued living seemed equally feasable propositions. The slow agony or the quick torpedo — we were too steeped in misery to care.

After an age the evening came and the heat declined. Hal looked at his watch.

"Exactly twenty-four hours since we set sail," he announced.

Twenty-four hours at approximately 12 knots — that would mean nearly 300 sea miles out of Benghazi, about half-way to our destination. Another twenty-four hours to endure!

At sunset we suffered a second emptying of latrine-drums and thus began the second night of Hell. The stench was worse than ever. So was the airlessness. Cries and groans were now almost continuous because the men's condition was deteriorating.

We thought of the slave-ships of old — how we sympathised with those unhappy wretches!

We should count our blessings.

"A good many of them died," reflected Hal . . .

We lay down and feigned sleep as on the first night, allowing our bodies to be trampled on without murmur or complaint . . .

In the end I must have slept from exhaustion for I opened my eyes to the morning light flooding in through the open hatches. I had missed the horror of the raising of the brimming latrine-drums . . .

"14th October, 1942. 36 hours in the prisonship," wrote Hal, taking advantage of the light.

The emptied latrines were lowered again and the hatches battened down.

"How you managed to sleep through all that, I'll never know, Ken."

"Maybe I passed out."

"But there was a terrible racket! One of the Indians was delirious, bawling at the top of his voice. I had to step over you to take him some water." Then changing the subject, "Where d'you think we are, Navigator?"

I calculated aloud:

"Thirty-six hours at between twelve and thirteen knots means we've gone about 450 nautical miles. Assuming that we're sailing north we should be in the Ionian Sea approaching the foot of Italy. The most likely ports are

Taranto and Brindisi. My guess is that they'll take us through the Straits of Otranto into the Adriatic."

Hal did some calculating of his own and said:

"At that rate we should arrive this evening. Thank God! One more day of this Hell is about all I could stand!" . . .

Throughout those last wearisome twelve hours we lay on the metal floor sweating, gulping in the foul air and aching in every limb.

At midday we sipped at the water-bottle surreptitiously and a little guiltily because few of the other POWs had any water left at all.

Among those hundreds of men that last afternoon the only movement was the pathetic procession to and from the latrines. Conversation was too much effort so that the only utterances were cries of pain . . .

The nightmare ended abruptly as most nightmares do.

Soon after five o'clock by Hal's watch, the throb of the engine steadied to slow, deliberate thumps. Presently it stopped altogether.

Followed a moment of tense silence. Then someone near the companion exclaimed:

"I'll bet it's a submarine!"

No sooner were the words out of his mouth than the hatches were opened and a voice shouted:

"Two men to empty buckets!"

A tall, thin rake of a man began to ascend towards the light. Half-way up he paused, looking down at us quizzically, a twinkle in his large brown eyes.

"Always lose me bloody bets — and get the filthy jobs!"

"Via! Via!" yelled the Italian at the top.

"Come on, Lofty, get on up!" urged a sandy-haired man on the lower rungs, "They haven't any depth-charges so they're going to use these buckets!"

"Cor!" said Lofty taking one hand off the rail to hold his nose. Whereupon he scrambled up on to the deck. The next moment his face re-appeared, eyes bulging with excitement.

"Land!" he cried, "We're just outside a harbour!" Then noticing the Fascist guard's ugly expression, he addressed his mate "Come on Bill. Let's get hauling!"

Bill Westaway, master-baker in civvy-street as we afterwards discovered, set to work with quiet efficiency. This time the latrine-drums were raised without any spillage whatsoever. We heard them being slid across the deck to be emptied. There followed a long and thorough hosing.

Some minutes later Lofty returned.

"If any of you fellers wants to go, you gotta tie a knot in it! We'll be stepping ashore in a few minutes!'

Presently Bill Westaway came into view. He was red-faced and perspiring having stowed the oil-drums single-handed.

As he descended the companion the engines started up again to drive the ship slowly forward into the harbour. The hatches remained open and we took deep breaths of the purer air. Hal timed the docking with his watch.

"Just fourteen minutes!" he announced as we felt the hull bump against the quayside fenders.

A snarling Fascist officer appeared at the hatch, flapping his arm.

"Now you all come out!" he ordered.

From somewhere there came a faint cheer and the longed-for exodus began.

At last Hal and I emerged into the blinding light to join the long line of ragged wretches shuffling forward across the deck and down the gang-plank onto the quayside.

Behind us was the harbour's narrow entrance; on either side of the main harbour, two little bays. Not far away we noticed a strange monument of brick and stone in the shape of a ship's rudder.

"Ugly isn't it?"

It was Bill Westaway following close at our heels.

"Quite the most horrible monument I've ever seen!" Hal declared.

One of the Fascist guards, noting our interest and wishing to show off his English, explained:

*"It is to make honour to the marinai of Italia, specialmente of Brindisi. Il Duce has commanded it."

"It's monstrous!" said Bill in a tone of enthusiastic admiration.

The Fascist was clearly delighted so I cadged a cigarette from him. Meanwhile Hal was sighting his watch on the sun. Then, gratefully accepting the gift, he pointed it up the coast.

"That's North," he announced, "Therefore this is the Adriatic Sea and the port definitely Brindisi."

As I walked down the plank I discerned a far more pleasing monument rising above the town, an ancient Roman pillar betokening the former glory of a great people.

It was many weeks later that I learnt that it marked the end of the Appian Way . . .

* To honour Italian sailors.

68

CHAPTER 11

Via Dolorosa

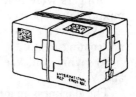

Behind a quayside wall we were halted, and the comedy of arranging us in groups and counting us was once again played. Because of the wall we could see no more than the masts and funnel of the hell-ship. That was enough. We never sought to discover its name; only to forget a time when we had been treated worse than cattle.

Once again the Indians had been grouped separately. When, with cries of "Via! Via!" from gesticulating guards, the column was persuaded to set forth, the Indians were made to follow us at a distance.

We trudged on, leaving harbour and town behind us, while the sun dipped crimson behind the dark hills. When anybody fell, his mates dragged him to his feet; and, hungry and exhausted as we all were, somehow we kept going until the banana-moon was bright among the stars.

By its light we saw that we were in the wide bed of a dried-up canal.

We were required to sit down in groups of seven. Hal and I were joined by Lofty and Bill and three Geordies.

"We're getting a Red Cross Food parcel!" announced Lofty.

Bill Westaway chuckled.

"Lofty always gets hold of the duff gen."

"I keeps me ears open, that's all! I got it from the Sergeant-Major who got it from the Eyeties. One parcel for every seven men, you'll see!"

A veil of cloud was spreading over the stars and the light fast fading. Above the murmur of voices, where shadowy uniformed figures moved busily, my ears detected the metallic sound of food tins being opened!

Opening up about a hundred Red Cross parcels was a lengthy procedure. Lofty smirked:

"Cor! I wish I'd had a bet on it!"

"You've got nothing left to bet with," remarked Bill, "In fact, none of us have."

"Hal there's got some cigs and Ken's got a comb."

"A tin of dog-ends and a few papers."

"This comb-case isn't going for stakes!" Hal and I spoke together, flourishing the items of property referred to.

It was dark by the time we seven received our parcel. One of the Geordies had managed to bring his mess-tin with him into captivity. His mate used the lid, while the rest of us ate from the cardboard box or its lid or the open tins therein contained.

It was a messy undertaking.

"Fingers were made before forks," quoth Hal, dipping into a toothsome mixture of raspberry jam, salmon and biscuit.

"We haven't any cutlery, but I don't suppose it'll matter as the vicar's not coming to tea!"

So saying, Bill Westaway scooped up a handful of Meat-and-Veg., ('M. and V.').

The darkness made every mouthful a surprise — unlikely mixtures of our parcel's contents. Doubtless a supply of parcels was stored in one of the quayside warehouses.

We didn't know it then but Red Cross Food parcels were ultimately to save our lives. Without them thousands of Allied POWs would have perished from malnutrition and starvation.

Each parcel, containing exactly the right proportions of protein and carbohydrates, was enough to sustain one man for one week. Actually receiving Red Cross Food parcels was quite another matter; in our experience an extremely rare occurrence, and, when it came to pass, the contents were usually to be shared between two or four men.

At the canal wall there was a tap where we queued through the night and early morning to fill our various containers. Afterwards we were able to make up some milk from the powder remaining in the "Klim"-tin. Alas! the greater portion of it had got itself mixed in with the salmon and jam and oats and "M and V" in the course of our ravenous fumbling!

Finally I lay down to sleep, grateful to be free from the nagging hunger-ache . . .

Almost immediately, it seemed, Hal was shaking me.

"Up you get, Ken! We're on the move."

The sun had already climbed above the film of cloud, promising another hot October day.

We were made to walk back to Brindisi the way we had come, only, as we drew near, branching away from the quayside.

Ahead of us a smoke-plume spewed into the morning air, hovered, dissipated, and was replaced by another and another at regular intervals. The accompanying retching sound interspersed with clanking indicated shunting in progress at the railway station.

As we shambled through a long street a loudspeaker suddenly began blaring out Fascist propaganda. A voice announced that this was a batch of newly-captured prigioneri. The British were starving; the poor condition of their soldiers was obvious. Fascist Italy was on the brink of a glorious victory!

Indeed we were a pitiful sight: some men had been too ill to partake of the Red Cross parcel, few of us had had any adequate feeding for weeks; most were ragged; all were unwashed and unshaven.

A pitiful sight — but no one pitied us! The onlookers hissed and jeered.

CHAPTER 11   VIA DOLOROSA

When any man stumbled or fell, they laughed. In their eyes there was only hate.

Such is the power of propaganda.

I tried to avoid looking at these duped people, fixing my eyes on that Roman column. Yet in remembering the Romans I found it hard to think of anything but the slaughter of Christians in the amphitheatre — their cruel streak . . .

It was a relief when at last we arrived at the railway station. No crowds here, in fact no other travellers in sight. As for the loudspeaker, it must have been switched off. Conversation, which had been hushed during the Parade of Captives, now started up again.

"D'you think there's a restaurant-car on the train?" asked Lofty, "I could just do with a bacon-egg-'n-chips!"

Westaway shook his head.

"Bad luck! You've just missed the Adriatic Express."

Lofty's answering obscenity was drowned by the engine whistle.

The cattle-trucks were jostling each other as we filed onto the platform; but by the time the first POWs reached the front truck the train was still, all doors open.

Without pause we were crammed in, about forty to a truck. The door was slammed and locked before we'd managed to fit our bodies into the limited floor space. We trod on each other and tripped over each other in the sudden darkness.

Westaway quipped, "Sorry Lofty! There's only sardines on the menu!"

Thereupon the trucks set up a hilarious jolting which can't have been all that funny for the last men boarding.

A derisive hoot from the engine, a final vicious slamming of doors, and the prison-train began to move.

We could tell we were out of the station because thin needles of light, penetrating one side of the truck, lit up the faces of some of our comrades.

"Navigator, what's our course?" demanded Hal.

"North obviously. The morning sun's to starboard."

Foul and cramped though the conditions were, they compared favourably with the steel-plated hold of the ship. If that had been Hell, this was Purgatory. This prison was at least partly of wood; the tiny crevices that let in light also let in air. Even more air circulated around the sliding door.

Once our eyes had become accustomed to the semi-obscurity some of us were able to take turns at viewing the landscape.

Hal discovered a small hole ideal for the purpose.

"High up there on the rocks," he said, "I can see the ruins of an old town. It's all stepped up in terraces."

Lofty, looking out on the other side, talked of vineyards.

Then Bill Westaway spied strange round buildings:

"Just like those little haystacks you see, like thatched cones. Only these are stone with white-tiled roofs."

71

ESCAPE FROM ASCOLI

As the day wore on the atmosphere inside the truck became increasingly oppressive. So many human beings in so confined a space gulping rather than breathing the befouled air. At every jolt one or other of the wounded would involuntarily cry out, at every jolt the inadequate latrine-bucket would slop over. Standing up to peer through the crevices required too much effort and, by the end of the first hour, even Lofty had huddled down on the floor to endure his misery privately. The stink became more and more nauseating.

After an eternity which by Hal's watch turned out to be only four hours, the train finally clanked to a halt. The door was thrust open by two surly-looking guards. I caught a glimpse of olive-groves and more distantly the sparkle of the Adriatic. Then one of the guards was prodding me with his rifle and I descended with haste onto the platform of Bari railway station.

Again we were led away for another Fascist parade of captives, loud-speakers churning out the same propaganda that we'd heard at Brindisi. We turned into a wide dusty avenue of palm-trees, lined with angry Baresi hooting and hissing and shaking their fists.

And it was a long, long walk — our Via Dolorosa!

Some of the crowd began pelting us with rotten fruit. The most hungry amongst us were sorely tempted to pick it up and eat it, but a timely word from a Black Watch sergeant prevented this final degradation.

"Dinna gie in, lads, and hold on to your self-respect!"

As he spoke a horse and carriage appeared at the top of the road. It moved at a gentle trot down beside the column of POWs, the driver idly holding his whip and looking away from the howling mob towards the spired top of a church tower.

Sitting bolt upright in the carriage was a white-haired old lady. She was weeping bitterly . . .

When we turned out of the street the loudspeaker was switched off. The narrow streets leading out of the town were deserted. Maybe it was siesta-time or maybe the non-Fascists deemed it prudent to stay indoors . . .

Bari POW Camp had been set up in a garden of olives. A large rectangle of convoluted barbed wire was divided into two smaller rectangles by a high fence. The fence itself was a network of rectangles formed by vertical and horizontal barbed wire strands.

On one side of the fence were white, pink-tiled buildings which had doubtless once served as farmstead and warehouses. On the other side was the olive-grove where a number of Italian-style tents huddled among the trees.

We were ordered to sit down in our groups outside the main gate — the entrance to the buildings compound.

Hal moved closed to me and spoke quietly.

"No chance of our getting away at present, Ken. This is definitely hostile territory."

I nodded my agreement, replying, "At the same time it's worth thinking about the townsfolk we didn't see."

72

Hal smiled, "Incorrigible optimist! If they were afraid to show their faces on the streets, they'd certainly be afraid to give us any kind of help."

At this he turned away from me and looked back at the groups of POWs behind us. Perhaps because of our eagerness to enlist in the boat-party at Benghazi, we now found ourselves in the leading group.

"Hullo, that's odd!" Hal's matter-of-fact mind was not often puzzled.

"What's up?" I asked. He shook his head in disbelief.

"The Indians!" he exclaimed, "We've lost the Indians!"

At that moment our group was required to stand up. As I got to my feet I too scrutinised the column of prisoners. It wasn't so long now and there wasn't an Indian in sight.

Somewhere on the route, perhaps near the quay, they'd creamed them off from the rest of us. It was not surprising because we knew that the enemy nourished hopes of weaning the Indians away from the Allied cause. They probably sought to organise them into working parties.

Anyway we couldn't imagine their having the slightest success with the Gurkhas! . . .

Once inside the main gate we were lined up in two separate files of twenty-five men on either side of the yard.

The Commandant appeared in full ceremonial dress, gold braid so dazzling and medal ribbons so vivid that he might have stepped straight out of a Gilbert and Sullivan opera.

He surveyed us disdainfully and muttered in the ear of his sergente who thereupon addressed us.

"We make now a ricerca before you enter the camp."

"Blimey!" groaned Lofty, "Another search! P'raps they think someone went shopping in the town when they weren't looking!"

The sergente continued:

"You will put all your clothez and belongings on the cortile in front of you. Then please to step back seexa passi."

Grumbling we stripped. The row of unshaven Adonisses opposite us managed six gigantic paces which took them into the shade of the buildings. We, like newly-sculptured clay statues, were left to bake in the mid-afternoon sun.

The searchers walked along the lines in pairs, one to examine our clothes, one to ensure that we were not concealing any items on our bodies.

Noticing that Hal's arms were pressed to his sides, the guard, a caporale, barked, "Raise your arms!" Hal obeyed. The guard nodded and came to me.

"Your ring, please. We keep safe for you!"

When I shook my head he grabbed my wrist and slid the wedding-ring from my finger. If ever in my life I could have committed murder it was in that moment. In the event I somehow fought back the tears welling up in my heart.

73

The caporale slid the comb from its case causing the tiny saw to fall to the ground.

"Ecco!" he cried triumphantly, picked up the saw and began examining Lofty's belongings.

"Thieving bastards!" exploded Lofty as the soldato semplice appropriated his wedding ring. The only item in his clothing was a small photo of his wife.

"Take your filthy mitts off that!"

Lofty's eyes were blazing.

"But of course!" sneered the caporale, releasing the photo so that it fluttered down onto the crumpled khaki shirt. Luckily there has no wind and it just lay there face upwards.

When the searchers moved on to Bill Westaway I breathed a sigh of relief. I'd really feared for Lofty! . . .

At last our group was told to dress. While we were so doing the Fascist thieves took their booty to the Commandant's office. There must have been a dozen rings and as many watches.

The sergente came forth again to assure us:

"Your objects of value are taken for safe keeping, you understand."

We understood! . . .

As we were marched out into the olive-grove so the next group was brought into the yard to be stripped and searched . . .

The whole charade took about an hour at the end of which we three hundred newly-arrived prisoners were sitting in the olive grove, our valuables, such as they were, piled on the Commandant's table.

The sergente addressed us once again:

"We 'ave very many prisoners here. However you will all find place in the tents — I think."

As he took his leave, we all moved in to greet the other POW's. The last group to be searched were now in front, with Hal and I well behind.

He walked close beside me and I noticed he was holding his fist clenched in front of him.

"Look Ken!" he whispered, opening his hand.

There in his palm was his gold wedding-ring together with his wrist-watch.

"But however did you manage it?"

His answer was so simple.

"I just held them in my hand," he replied, "they peered and pried everywhere else but overlooked the obvious."

CHAPTER 12

Hoppers in the straw

By the time we reached the tents all the places were taken.

A tall, lantern-jawed man clapped me on the shoulder.

"Don't worry. They'll rustle up another tent domani. Expect you can take one more night in the open?"

"Of course. It's a fine night."

"Tell you what — I know where I can borrow a blanket!"

He grinned, hurried towards a cluster of tents and, before we'd had time to speak, was back, a large grey blanket draped over his arm.

As I gratefully accepted it he thrust forward a welcoming hand.

"By the way, my name's Davey — Reverend Davey — but please call me "Peter" after "Widdicombe Fair', you know!"

"Sergeant Ken de Souza — RAF observer."

"Flight-Sergeant Harold Curtois — RAF pilot."

It was a novel experience — shaking hands under a blanket!

Peter informed us that he'd been at Bari a fortnight, that the feeding was just tolerable but that we were unlikely to receive any Red Cross parcels as it was only a transit camp.

"When we get to a permanent camp we should have a food parcel every week, not to mention the bulk parcels of medical aid, cigarettes and so on. Now do please excuse me! I've promised to have a chat with old Chris. He's very depressed. One of the few people to receive a letter and it only brought bad news. See you chaps in the morning. Sleep well!" . . .

As the shadows lengthened we sought out a suitable piece of ground — flat, free of stones and, despite the tread of many feet, still retaining some grass. We stretched out the blanket and Hal placed his satchel underneath it just where he expected our heads would be. Then we lay down at opposite ends and, holding the edges, rolled towards each other.

Our subsequent sleep was due more to our exhaustion than to the comfort of the situation. However it was possible for either of us to get up without disturbing the other . . .

I awoke to see Hal, propped up against a nearby wooden pole, writing in his diary. On the top of the pole was mounted a powerful lamp. There were several of these lamp-poles dotted about the orchard to enable the sentries to have a clear view of all our activities.

The sentry-boxes were on stilts and in the one opposite us a green-uniformed guard was lounging half-asleep, his weapon or weapons quite out-of-sight.

"Friday, Sixteenth of October, 1942," read out Hal, "First day in POW Transit Camp at Bari."

I unrolled myself from the blanket which I then folded and carried over to Hal.

We sat upon it as the dawn-light crept into the olive-grove; as the silver-green leaves began to tremble in the breath of morning, as the first bees began to murmur, as the undertones of men's voices drifted from the tents.

Peter Davey came striding towards us, shaven and beaming, spruce except for wisps of straw clinging to his clothing.

"You chaps have a good night? — That's marvellous! You know, we've got to look after you I think you're the only RAF people here."

We expressed our surprise, got up and handed back what I suspected was his own blanket. He waved aside our thanks and continued:

"Told Chris about you. Cheered him up no end and he's looking forward to meeting you. That's what one has to do, you see — give these chaps something to look forward to."

"But how can we help?" I asked.

"Because you're RAF, that's why. He grew up at Farnborough in the days of the Royal Flying Corps. Wanted to be a pilot but failed the medical, so went off with his brother to Aldershot and got himself into the Army. That was the year before the War. So just talk to him about flying, life in the RAF, any stories you know."

Hal rubbed his beard thoughtfully.

"We'd be glad to, but at the moment we look more like a couple of scarecrows than RAF glamour-boys."

Peter laughed.

"I've thought of that!" He delved into his battledress pocket and brought forth a safety-razor. "This should tidy you two up, I managed to get it smuggled in. Sorry there's only the one blade!"

When we tried to thank him, he changed the subject:

"We all get paid today — POW pay at five lire per week."

The news that POW's were entitled to any pay at all amazed us.

"Something to do with the Geneva Convention," explained Peter, "but five lire isn't much. Worth about a shilling. We buy cakes from Bari to supplement the meagre diet."

"Surely we aren't allowed to visit the town?" exclaimed Hal disbelievingly.

"No, one of the Italians goes down every Saturday. I believe the shop belongs to his brother."

We guessed then how Peter had come by the razorblade.

Smiling, he continued:

"Those little Genoese cakes cost three lire each. But the arrangement suits us very well. You see, the patissier and his brother aren't true Fascists and

76

they're convinced the Allies are going to win the war. So in order to keep in our good books, they keep us up-to-date with the war-news!" . . .

Peter Davey was right about the meagre diet: a small hunk of bread accompanied by a much smaller piece of meat. Some days, instead of meat there was a slice of cheese; some days, neither. One happy day we each had an apple!

Basking in the warm October sun, we were aware of, but not yet tortured by the pangs of hunger.

Peter was also right about our being provided with a tent. A couple of smiling soldati marched in with a bundle of rods. It took them about three minutes to fit them together to make the oblong frame. Back they scampered to fetch a bundle of groundsheets which they dextrously buttoned together and spread over the frame. After pegging the skirts of the contraption to the ground, they departed beckoning us to follow. At first we mistook their gesture as waving us away, but when we paused it became a frantic pantomime.

They led us to the straw-store, then left us to make several journeys with armfuls of straw until the tent-floor was well covered. Our last journey was to collect a blanket each. Immediately we had passed through the compound gate, the Fascist guard locked it, scowled at us and spat into the dust.

Later we received our pay and pooled it to buy three Genoese cakes. As neither meat nor cheese appeared that weekend they were a godsend — enough, together with watery skilly, to see us through.

On Saturday evening we walked in the olive orchard, taking time to chat with all the "old lags" we met. Thus we verified that none of our crew were here. We were the only RAF types at P.G.75! However we did meet Lofty and his friend, Bill Westaway.

Lofty jerked his thumb towards their previous night's abode.

"It pongs in there somethin' 'orrible — ten of us like bloody sardines!" he muttered.

Bill Westaway reached down under his shirt collar to scratch the middle of his back.

"That's not the worst of it," he grimaced, "The straw's filthy and teeming with hoppers."

"By all means come and sleep on our clean straw," invited Hal.

With a heartfelt "Thanks fellers!" Lofty turned and made off back to his previous tent. Bill grinned appreciatively, winked and gave the thumbs-up sign before following him.

We continued walking until curfew. On re-entering our tent we found Bill and Lofty both fast asleep . . .

For me that night sleep was hard to come by. I sat grieving over the theft of my wedding-ring. The Italians who had captured me could never have been capable of such a despicable crime . . .

Oh for a photo of my love! . . .

Suddenly I was startled to hear the voice which has sustained me in the desert:

"For Pete's sake, Ken, snap out of it and go to sleep!"

Obediently I lay down and, like Hal and Bill and Lofty, I closed my eyes . . .

The next night the Bari fleas discovered the new tent, romping in its sweet straw and attacking us incessantly from all quarters. Now and again one of us would sit up and, by the light of the outside lamp, carry out five minutes' frantic execution. But it was a mere drop in the pool: we hadn't a hope of keeping pace with their fantastic birthrate!

On the Sunday Peter Davey held a religious service. We sang the words of the hymns from memory. After a period of silent prayer, we sat down while Peter chatted to us. It was so unlike any sermon I'd ever heard from the pulpit — just simple and direct, a friend talking to his friends. He made it clear to us that, despite our unpleasant situation, we had each so much to thank God for.

Not until he had finished did the flea-afflicted congregation remember that there were places crying out to be scratched.

During the blessing, it needed great will-power to keep hands together in the attitude of prayer! . . .

Two days later in the evening Hal wrote in his diary "Tuesday, 20th October, 1942. Today we had a Disinfestation Parade. Brrh!"

Quite abruptly that morning clouds had appeared with the onset of a cool wind.

We had stood around on the cortile, unclothed and shivering, while our bundled clothing was treated in a steamer resembling Stevenson's "Rocket." It was left in there just long enough to make it damp and to activate any fleas that might have been resting after their night's labours.

Receiving it back, we were required to open it out, shake it and wear it again. It was like dressing up in stale-smelling boiled-pudding-cloths! Thus we returned to our compound to make way for the next lucky people.

On the way back we met the soldati who had put up our tent. I performed my smoking mime, smiled and thereby received a cigarette from one of them. Although it was only a despised "Nazionali" Hal was delighted for by this time he was very low on dogends. Somehow, throughout our captivity, I was always able to procure a smoke for Hal when it was most needed.

There were men whose craving for cigarettes surpassed their craving for food. It was a pitiful plight. In the worst days they starved, became skeletons and some of them died. All because they traded every scrap of food for cigarettes.

Fortunately Hal's will-power enabled him to overcome such temptations . . .

As we walked through the orchard next day we came across POWs gathering the olive leaves. Some of the trees were already completely stripped!

CHAPTER 12   HOPPERS IN THE STRAW

"We gotter smoke summat, mate!" protested a bare-headed man astride one of the branches. His forage-cap was already stuffed with leaves!

The sequel came to pass exactly one week later: about a hundred men were stricken with yellow jaundice and the Italians presented us with a bill for many thousand lire for damage to the olive trees.

However by then we were all agog with the news which had come to us via the carrier of cakes. The Eighth Army had broken through at El Alamein. The remnants of Rommel's forces were in full retreat across North Africa.

CHAPTER 13

Cattle in transit

The clouds which had long been gathering, dispersing, then standing off and re-grouping, finally burst upon us.

Around three o'clock in the morning an earsplitting crash of thunder signalled the attack. Sheets of water slapped down onto our tent-roofs bulging them inwards and streaming through the buttonholes.

When Lofty pushed out one of the bulges the displaced pool emptied itself through the nearest buttonholes, drenching the bundle below. The bundle happened to be Bill Westaway, tight-wrapped in his blanket seeking in vain to withdraw himself from the chaos.

"Idiot!" gurgled Bill.

"Sorry mate. I thought the tent was caving in!"

"I don't give a damn if it does! Then you'd all be as wet as I am." So saying, the soggy bundle curled up in his misery like a disturbed woodlouse.

Not another word was spoken as we all jockeyed for position on the ever-diminishing patches of dry straw.

The only redeeming feature was respite from the fleas now doubtless taking refuge deep in the straw.

When morning came the saturated ground was steaming but the sky was clear and innocent.

It was my turn to call on Chris, Hal having chatted with him the previous day.

However hungry we were, however sick or maltreated, our greatest torment was anxiety for wives and families at home. They too were in the firing-line. One of my squadron friends had told me that his mother had been "bombed out" four times! She'd had five different addresses in Tilbury in a hectic fortnight, miraculously coming through unscathed, though grumbling about not being able to wash the dust out of her hair!

Of course letters were censored and such news wouldn't reach us. But most shattering of all was the kind of news that had got through to Chris. After five years of marriage his wife had "found somebody else" whom she loved dearly and by whom she was pregnant.

"We couldn't have a nipper, you see, not her and me. Don't know for why but it never worked. He turned his face away as he handed me a Polyfoto portrait. She was a lively-looking buxom girl. "Taken just before we was married."

I pretended not to notice his choking sob, and launched into a yarn about barrage balloons and the frightening whine which warned us when we flew near them. Finally he responded with tales about World War I observation balloons.

I realised that his wife must have been several years younger than he . . .

On Saturday, 31st of October we left Bari. It was early morning and the streets were quiet.

As at Brindisi goods trucks awaited us at the railway station. Once we had been crammed in, all four hundred of us, the doors were locked and another slow, clattering journey began.

There were no tiny crevices or spy-holes in this truck. It was hot and airless and dark. Conversation died for breathing became an effort. I lay propped against the side, a rivet thrusting deeper at every jolt into my vertebrae. I tried to concentrate on the vague rectangle of light around the door. When it flickered I guessed at the features interposed between train and sun. A tree or a telegraph-pole? A fence or a row of buildings? Or, when the sound became hollow as in a vault, maybe a tunnel or a station?

The remorseless rhythm became part of me — a throbbing in my head beating out an eternity. The frame of light faded, the pain in my back dulled, the throbbing slowed and mercifully ceased. Happy release! So this was how it all ended, the fever of life over — just an abiding silence, complete relaxation and peace . . .

"Ken, are you OK now?" Hal's voice drifted down to me. He was gripping my shoulders and shaking me.

I opened my eyes, then shielded them with my hands from the blaze of light. The truck door was open.

"Christ, I thought you were a gonner!" he exclaimed.

"Hal! Ken! Come on mates! Give a chap a hand!"

It was Bill Westaway down on the track with the emptied latrine-bucket. A guard stood menacingly behind him. I crawled across and with Hal stooping beside me, helped pull him aboard. Them we two scrambled down to water the sleepers.

Once out in the fresh air I came completely to my senses and paused a moment admiring the scene before me — orchards, vineyards and modest stone-built farmhouses; and beyond them, tranquil and sparkling, the Adriatic Sea.

"The railway runs north-west," Hal announced, squinting at the hands of his watch which he'd duly orientated with the sun.

"Parallel to the coast," I noted, adding, "Nearly five hours travelling, say 150 miles, could put us north of the Foggia peninsula: That'll be the only part where the coast doesn't run north-west."

Hearing us talking and maybe wondering at Hal's pose with his wrist in front of his face, a Fascist Sergeant yelled at us, pointing his rifle.

Prudently we made our way back across the rails. As we did so we caught our first glimpse of the lower slopes of the Appenines, rising slate-blue into the brilliant sky. In the foreground the undulating landscape was a clean patchwork of vivid colours — yellow and green and russet, quite different from the flat, olive-blotched dusty country around Bari.

The rifle safety-catch clicked. We hastened back to Lofty and Bill who were waiting to haul us up into the cattle-truck.

It amused the guards to hustle us and several of our companions had been prodded with rifle-butts. They slammed the doors violently and we were consigned once more to the jolting, the darkness, and the near-suffocation.

"Blimey! this lot hates our guts!" exclaimed Lofty.

He was right, or nearly so. So far in this country everybody seemed to hate us. But I remembered the old lady weeping in her carriage, the two smiling soldati who had put up our tent, and the fighting men who had captured me.

"The Fascists do," I said, "They're the thugs but I don't think all the people are like that. After all, Italy is a Christian nation."

Bill chuckled:

"An optimist to the end is our Ken!" and Hal added, "Navigator's prerogative!"

We fell silent after that, either busy with our own thoughts or sleeping or feigning sleep.

I achieved that same detached semi-conscious state which dulled discomfort and hastened the passing of time. According to Hal it was over four hours before we once more ground to a halt.

The door opened. I took a few seconds to get used to the light and to realise that we were at a station. Came the sounds of other doors being slid open, shouts of "Via! Via!"; and, rising above the engine's sighing, a growing murmur from our fellow-prisoners tumbling out onto the platform.

Bill and Lofty helped me down. Then the rest of our truckload followed. The engine gasped with relief and lugged the line of empty trucks out of the station. On the opposite platform we read the name-board:

"PORTO SAN GIORGIO."

Beyond the white-walled, pink-roofed railway building were other taller white buildings with pink roofs. All was neat and scrupulously clean.

The murmur of voices around me suddenly rose in a crescendo of excitement. Hal nudged me.

"Ken, quit day-dreaming! Look! Down there at the end of the platform!"

I looked, and was touched by what I saw.

A group of about a dozen civilians, men and women, had set up a trestle-table on the platform. On the table was placed a barrel of wine which they had already broached.

A smiling black-clad woman was beckoning the POWs. Her companion, also in black, was pouring glasses of wine. Two other women were laying out glasses on the long table. I noticed that all the women were barefoot.

The heavy-booted men, having erected the table, appeared to be scrutinis-ing our Fascist guards who, incredible as it may seem, were shrinking back into the shadows obviously loath to be recognised.

ESCAPE FROM ASCOLI

Maybe they thought that, if the impossible came to pass and the Axis lost the war, it might not be beneficial to be recognised as an active Fascist.

We shambled forward to take the wine — I don't think there was a man amongst us who was not overwhelmed by this, the first positive kindness anyone in this country had shown us. Many wept.

It was our first encounter with the contadini of the province of Ascoli Piceno.

These wonderful folk had abiding love in their hearts and compassion for fellow human-beings in distress.

It took a long time for everybody to take the wine — not mild sweet wine as for communion, but acidic vino crudo. But we received it as a symbol of love and thereby a holy sacrament.

Finally the peasant women placed on their heads little haloes of cloth upon which they balanced wine-barrels or ewers or trays of glasses. The men carried away the trestles.

Their chatter flowed away out of the station to merge with the growl of heavy traffic on the autostrada which ran beside the railway.

We stood motionless gazing at the empty platform-end, a huddle of poor wretches who had just seen a vision . . .

The Fascist guards swaggered forth again to herd us across to the station-yard and into the waiting road-trucks. We were just as crowded and uncomfortable as in the train, the guards were just as surly; but the wine episode had cheered us and all our privations now seemed more bearable.

The trucks turned right, going northwards for a few hundred yards along the autostrada before branching left into a small country road leading inland.

An open German staff car roared past us in a cloud of dust but the grey-uniformed officers didn't deem us worthy of a glance. A few minutes later we overtook a colourful wooden cart drawn by an aged horse. The blue-shirted driver was dozing and the horse might have been deaf and blind for all the notice he took of our growling engines.

That was all the traffic we saw upon the road. With my back to the cab I watched the cart until it moved out-of-sight behind a long stone building whose windows shone in the late afternoon sun.

The guards eyed me menacingly as I turned to contemplate the landscape ahead.

What I saw was breathtaking in its beauty. In the foreground lay bright sunlit fields and orchards; beyond them sudden little hills crowned with white buildings deep-chequered with shadow; and beyond again, rising towards the sun, the magnificent peaks of the Appenines.

Up there the interplay of light and shadow was pure magic — Indian-ink clefts and caverns lurked amongst molten-gold crags of fire. Like many of my companions I'd never looked upon a mountain-range in all my life; like them I was spellbound.

The road began to descend, and across the valley the fields were blue with flax.

CHAPTER 13   CATTLE IN TRANSIT

Below us we saw blocks of warehouses built with geometrical precision. Each block comprised about ten adjoining sections, each section having a curved pink roof. The effect was of a long undulating course of tiles. These blocks flanked a central building whose roof was angled or stepped. We guessed this would be the factory, if factory there were.

As we drew closer the height of those warehouses became apparent — tall buildings with window-spaces set high in brilliant white walls.

As usual it was Lofty who voiced the realisation that had dawned on us.

"This is it, mates — our new home! Never saw so much barbed wire and just look at all them sentry-boxes perched up there!"

CHAPTER 14

P.G.70 at Monte Urano

The rectangle within which buildings and grounds were contained was bounded on its two lengths by a high wall; the widths taken up with what appeared to be an Admin. block at one end, a dense barrier of barbed wire at the other.

The trucks halted outside the admin block where the outer wall was comparatively low. As soon as we set foot on the ground, green-uniformed soldiers hustled us into the camp proper. It all happened astonishingly quickly. Only a few minutes after being crammed in the trucks we were on the wrong side of a tall forbidding fence and a tall gate had clanged to behind us.

We found ourselves in a paved courtyard flanked by offices and storerooms. Several of the old lags were watching but none ventured into the reception area. Two men were waiting to receive us: the grey-haired Commandante who stood modestly aside as a benevolent-looking Warrant-Officer strolled forward.

"Welcome, lads, to P.G.70., POW Camp for other ranks. My name's Atkinson and I'm the Camp Leader. We'll do our best for you but I'm afraid things aren't too good just at present."

"But the Red Cross —" began Hal.

With a wry smile Warrant-Officer Atkinson shook his head.

"Sorry! They haven't discovered us yet. However, the main thing is to get yourselves organised right away. I want each group to choose a Leader and a Deputy. They will be responsible for distributing meals and anything else that becomes available."

"I propose Hal here and Ken!" piped up Lofty; and Bill Westaway, anxious not to be chosen himself, seconded enthusiastically:

"The two RAF fellers — we couldn't do better."

It was as though it had been pre-arranged: the whole thing was settled before either of us could draw breath and while the other group elections were only just getting started.

Meanwhile the outer gate had closed and the line of trucks was already threading its way out of the valley. We watched them until a shout from one of the guards indicated that, group elections having been completed, they were ready to show us to our quarters. We followed them past the central hall to a high concrete building that was once a warehouse, now

"P.G.70 — Compound 2". The next warehouse. Compound 1, we were told, already contained two thousand men.

On the concrete floor stood rows of tiered slatted wooden beds, about half of which, being unoccupied, were just bare wood.

The other half belonged to the "old lags," some of whom were sitting in groups on the bottom bunks, some just lying on their straw palliasses.

Voices crying out of the shadows asked similar questions to those put to us when we'd entered the camp at Benghazi.

"What's the news, mates?"

"Got any good rumours?"

This time we were able to give more encouraging answers.

Hal spoke to the nearest "old lag".

"We broke through at Alamein a week ago and Jerry's in retreat."

"Man that's smashing! He turned to his mate. D'ye hear that? The push has started!"

"Aye, I hear it reet enough," retorted the other without enthusiasm, adding, "Reckon it's nowt but another bloody rumour!"

When I explained to him how we had got the news from a reliable source at Bari, he observed sarcastically:

"So you two Raff fellers wasn't actually at Alamein yourselves!" . . .

We staked claim to a bunk and laid there our meagre possessions.

Compound Two wash-house was opposite the barrack-block entrance. The roofed brick-and-tile hut made a welcome change from the open earth-pits of Mersa, Benghazi, Brindisi and the Bari olive-grove. Nevertheless the facilities were quite unlike anything we had ever come across before.

The closet was a hole in the concrete floor with foot-places strategically arranged on either side. The performer was expected to insert his feet in the grooves and squat. The first experience was the worst: with practice it became easier to keep one's balance.

"It's the natural position," proclaimed Bill Westaway, who in his time had been a gymnast, "Much better for you!"

Washing was an exercise in patience; shaving, for the few who possessed a safety-razor, virtually impossible. A pipe ran above each long row of metal basins. By means of cupping hands below one of the skewer-sized holes in the pipe, it was possible to collect water which spurted, dribbled or dripped therefrom according to the fluctuations of the water-pressure.

The water was spurting forth merrily until the moment that I stretched forth my hands. Then abruptly it stopped! I moved to the next hole. That dried up too, but water again issued from the original one. I returned there to collect as many drips and dribbles as were needed to wash my hands and dampen my face . . .

Warrant Officer Atkinson was waiting at Number 2 Compound entrance to take our group to the store to fetch palliasses and straw.

As we passed in front of the central hall our feet thudded across a large iron weighbridge platform — reminder of the peacetime function of this place.

"It was a flax factory," explained Atkinson, "They weighed the truckloads here as they came in."

While our group — Group 57 — were collecting empty palliasses and rations of straw, the Camp Leader waited at the door with us.

"Things are grim at present, Sergeant Curtois. We're supposed to get a bowl of soup each day plus a bread ration with a slice of cheese or meat. In practice the soup is usually thin and watery, we often miss a day with the bread, cheese or meat issues are erratic. Most of the men are suffering from malnutrition. I rely on you to let me know of any extreme cases in your group."

"Is there a medical room on the camp?" asked Hal.

"We have a room," replied Atkinson grimly, "and we have a first-class Medical Officer, Major Parkes, senior officer on the camp. But we've scarcely any medical supplies —"

"Can't the Major persuade the Italian Commandante —?" I began.

"Yes, if anybody can, Doc. Parkes can. But there's nowt to be had except maybe a double-loaf for a couple of weeks." Then changing the subject, "Now when all the men have taken back their bedding, I'd like you to bring your group round here again and issue skillybowls and spoons." . . .

The next morning we made up the roster of "skilly-carriers" — two men each day to carry the soup-tureen to the serving-point allocated to Group 57. This was done by means of a stout pole passed through the tureen's carrying-handles.

Precisely at midday the camp bugler sounded the call to the cookhouse.

The carriers departed and all the groups queued up with their earthenware bowls at the various distribution points.

Presently our pair returned, shuffling uncertainly on either side of the tureen of steaming slop.

"Look out, you're spilling it!" shouted someone angrily.

They lowered it to the ground with the utmost care.

The ladle was a Red Cross *"Klim"-tin fastened to a wooden handle. The tin proved that food parcels had at some time arrived here.

"Probably a bulk consignment sent on from some other depot," said Hal as I set about stirring the pottage with the long stick provided, "Okay, that'll do. We'll try it now."

He scooped out a Klimtinful, then poured it slowly back. It was a vegetable soup.

"It's halfway between stodge and skilly," he diagnosed, emptying a scoopful into the first man's bowl.

By the time he'd served twenty men the vegetable content was sinking.

* Powdered milk-tin which held more than a pint.

89

"Come on mate! Stir it up!" chorused the POWs next in line. Hal paused while I obeyed.

We had yet to learn the art of maintaining an even consistency throughout the serving. More often than not the last man's soup was the thickest.

Later that afternoon Hal and I sat on the lower bunk chatting to the two old lags on the lower bunk opposite. We formed a tight little crew for the distance between the rows was no more than three feet.

"I'm Jim Mackay, and this is my oppo John." It was the auburn-haired POW who made the introductions.

"How long 've you bin in the bag, hinny?" John was dark-eyed, dark-haired and longer in the face than his friend.

"Five weeks," I replied.

"We was taken at Tobruk months an' months ago. Mind, I've lost some weight since then."

It was true. His cheekbones stuck out and, through the open vee of his khaki shirt, I glimpsed his ribs. He went on, "Jim here's better padded than me. He gets a double-loaf, you see, because he does the barbering."

Jim turned on him. "Man, you're always welcome to share, y'knaw that."

"I wouldna," retorted John, "You need the strength to do your job. We'd be a lot o' scarecrows else!"

"Anyways," remarked Jim, "it doesn't look as if anyone's getting any bread this day."

"Pane domani!" sighed John, "Mebbe yous chaps haven't heard that before. It's the camp motto — bread, sometime never!"

It followed that, if there were no bread, no meat or cheese would be issued either . . .

Later Hal and I took a walk around the "garden" — a flat dusty patch where half a dozen slender trees clung tenuously to life. It was bordered by a path which in turn was bordered by the trip-wire at the foot of the outer wall and some four feet away from it.

The stranded trip-wire was stretched about three feet above the ground. It was the wire of death: the sentinelle, in their boxes high above, had orders to shoot any prisoner who touched it.

Most of the men we met were thin and weak and unsteady in their walking. There were others in the barracks, we were told, lying on their beds unable to walk.

"Escape is out of the question until the Red Cross food parcels arrive," declared Hal.

I had to agree with him but pointed out that we were likely to receive some help from the peasants if we did manage to get out of the camp.

"What we must do now is to prepare for our escape." As Hal looked puzzled, I explained:

"Remember the German who was planted on us at Mersa? Well, there'll almost certainly be a plant here — or at least the Fascists will have some intelligence system. I reckon it's important that we give the impression that

90

we don't give a damn about escaping. Let them look upon us as obedient well-behaved prisoners."

Hal nodded, and stopped to roll a dog-end cigarette.

"My last fag-paper," he said, "and no one's mentioned a shop here in P.G.70 — Good Lord! What's that noise?"

The noise came from the other side of the garden where a couple of dozen men were gathered in the shade of a tree. It was an accordeon, its player young, fair-haired and broadly smiling. We could see that smile right across the garden — an infectious George-Formby sort of smile!

Two POWs stopped beside us to say:

"That's Fred Hill, the Salvation Army chap. He's a card! Why not come over and join us?"

As we drew near, the congregation began to sing John Bunyan's hymn:

"He who would valiant be
'Gainst all disaster."

Fred welcomed us with a wide grin as, with a full heart, we did indeed join the singing.

The companion who had sustained me in the desert seemed close-by at that moment . . .

Roll calls were held morning and late afternoon. Groups assembled in the area fronting the central hall and the Italian Commandant, Colonello Papa, would occasionally take up position on the weighbridge platform to watch proceedings.

It was exactly the same system as at Bari except that here one or two of the old lags had perfected the trick of surreptitiously moving into a nearby group to confuse the issue.

"Trenta-sei, quaranta, quaranta-quattro," called out the soldati counting in fours, "quarant-otto, — be? cinquanta-due!" Where had the two extra men come from? The neighbouring groups were correct because the visitors had already been counted!

On a fine day it was pleasant to stand there and look beyond and above the central hall at the steep-sloping colourful fields; at the village of Fermo shining on the crest of its little hill; at the awesome grandeur of the distant mountains. But not many fine days remained in the month of November.

A few mornings later I awoke to a confusion of sounds — splashing and howling, shrieking and swearing. The splashing I identified as rainwater overflowing the guttering; the howling was the wind striking the high-set open rectangles as it threw water over the nearest top-bunks; the swearing came ripe from the drenched occupants whose beds shrieked as they were scraped across the concrete floor as far as possible away from the "windows".

It rained, and it rained, and it rained! Day and night it rained incessantly so that the garden and parade area became a black, sloppy morass. Roll calls became a misery for guards and prisoners alike, but Colonello Papa in those days of deluge was nowhere to be seen. Strangely, the counting was always correct first time!

ESCAPE FROM ASCOLI

Alas! the rain did nothing to expedite the arrival of Red Cross parcels while the Italian rations became less substantial than ever. The soup got more watery every day, and as for bread there was always an excuse for its non-arrival. *"Pane domani!" we muttered hopefully.

One morning Hal was too weak to get up from his bunk. Therefore during the next three days I took over the running of Group 57. It brought about an immediate change of fortune.

My first day as leader saw the arrival of the first letters to be received by any of our men, the first post to come in at P.G.70 for many weeks. We had an issue of bread AND meat, and the soup turned out to be sheer stodge from top to bottom!

No post the next day but a Red Cross bulk parcel got through to the camp. We all received new socks and there were khaki shirts for those most in need! Also a few thick khaki pullovers. The stodge held up and we were given cheese with our bread.

The third day Hal was on his feet again but still rather unsteady so I remained in charge.

We had a medium soup, the bread and cheese came in and, incredibly, another Red Cross bulk parcel this time real English cigarettes!

"Three cheers for Ken!" cried out Lofty, "He sure is some group leader!" There were even those who wanted me to continue but I knew that there could be no better leader than Hal — no one more responsible, no one more resourceful.

Of course, when Hal did eventually take over, the soup turned to skilly, bread and meat were promised for domani and Atkinson said he understood the bulk parcels we'd received had been sent down from the camp at Macerata.

"I don't think the Red Cross have any idea there's a big POW camp here at Monte Urano," he declared.

"What about the letters?" objected Hal.

"If you notice they were forwarded on from Bari," replied the Camp Leader gloomily.

The rain ceased, but after a couple of sunny days, cool showery weather set in.

Most of us were now suffering from malnutrition. One morning I awoke too feeble to get down from my bunk. I huddled miserably in my blanket, shivering, trying to come to terms with the aching emptiness in my belly.

Hal laid his blanket on top of mine. His voice sounded far away.

I slept or lost consciousness — until the midday skilly-bugle sounded. I opened my eyes to see the faces of Hal, John and Jim peering over the foot of my top bunk.

"It's all reet for some lying in their pits all morning!" Jim chided.

"No doubt ye'll be coming down to take the soup?"

* Bread tomorrow!

92

Then the three of them helped me down to the lower bunk.

"Now Sir, gie us your bowl and it will be my pleasure to serve you the soup o' the day!" Jim Mackay's blue eyes twinkled as he spoke and John murmured, "Dinna fret, Ken. It happens to us all — mebbe me next time. It's just the bloody malnutrition. Yous'll be better after the skilly." He gave me a friendly wink and followed the others out.

I noticed that the sun was shining.

My soup was thick and three-quarters filled my bowl. It was only after the three of them had finished — long before me, of course — that I realised why!

That was how we survived the winter and early spring. Whenever a man was too ill to walk his mates cared for him until he was on his feet again. It was vital to have at least one good mate. Sadly, some POWs did not survive.those weeks of near-starvation. Exactly how many men died we never knew; rumour put the number at more than twenty.

What we did know was the importance of the will to survive. Malnutrition could lead to a state of inertia when it became too much trouble to make the effort. If the sufferer, like Chris at Bari, was beset with other anxieties, he could so easily give up the struggle. Mostly, the real problem was psychological.

While some men as the caring Peter Davy and the ever-cheerful Fred Hill ranked high in our esteem, we came to know one man whose spiritual influence transformed the whole camp. He worked miracles, restoring hope to the hopeless, life to the dying. His own privations he ignored, dedicating himself completely to the welfare of others. His quiet good-humour was unshakeable.

Such a man was the Reverend Douglas Thompson.

Of slight build, hair thinning at the temples, bespectacled, ascetic in features — yet there was such power in this man that the sick and the lame would get up from their bunks and stagger out into the garden to hear him speak.

Abstruse theological dissertations were not for him: every word he uttered related to real life and real people. He would stand in front of one of those spindly trees apparently speaking quietly, yet his every word was audible even at the back of the vast congregation, audible and meaningful, and helpful.

He sought out any man who was in despair and, quietly chatting with him, somehow re-kindled hope. In this way he worked miracle upon miracle! He managed to obtain a supply of slim New Testament bibles. Soon after I'd recovered from my bout of malnutrition-weakness, he gave me one.

"The Fascists must have been seeking the Holy Truth!" he joked, indicating the inside cover along which the Italian searchers had made a diagonal cut . . .

From the last week of November onwards Red Cross supplies began to trickle through to P.G.70, bulk parcels mostly. We received letter-forms to write home once a week. The families of non-smokers must have wondered at the constant request for cigarettes. With cigarettes a man could buy bread from those whose craving for a smoke was even greater than their desire for food.

Tragically, because of pilfering, scarcely any personal parcels ever reached us. The tremendous sacrifices made by our families in times of rationing were almost always in vain. At best a POW might receive the pathetic remnants of his despoiled parcel.

If there had not been better protection for official Red Cross food parcels the death toll at P.G.70 would have been much greater. Prison camp rations on their own were scandalously inadequate.

The Red Cross food parcel contained precisely the right balance of nutriments to sustain one person for one week. The only occasion of such a luxury was on Christmas Day 1942. Then one man, indulging to excess, ate a whole pound-tinful of steak-and-kidney pudding for his dinner. We heard that he died on Boxing Day.

By early December we had gathered enough Red Cross food-tins to manufacture cooking-stoves. In their crudest form these were just Klim-tins with handles — effective kettles none-the-less. Hal being the practical man he was, devised a contraption with oven, damper control and two "rings" to fit Klim-tins.

From the opened-out tins we made metal plates, bashing them scientifically with conveniently flat stones. The plates we then turned over at the edges so that they would interlock. Long and patient pounding made an effective join. In this way we built the frame of the thing to the specifications of Hal's blue-print. Stone-age fashion we cut various components of various shapes which Hal ingeniously assembled.

Fuel supply was a constant preoccupation. Scraps of cardboard from the Red Cross boxes and elsewhere, twigs from the trees, straw from the palliasses, slats from our wooden beds — such was the miscellany upon which the combustion of our "Smokey-Joes" depended. Best of all were embers from the cookhouse — a low building on the north side of our compound, like a long shelter lacking an outer wall.

It needed only one POW in the group to succeed in cadging embers: the precious fire could then, like the Olympic torch, be passed from man to man. The final victory over darkness was yet to come; meanwhile for POWs every meal was a battle won in the quest for survival.

On our Plain of Marathon — the "brew patch" — the little fires were kindled. Men knelt humbly on the dark earth breathing life into their cookers or wafting hopefully with pieces of cardboard.

At first our culinary activities were restricted to brewing, often re-using old ersatz coffee-grouts and/or tea-leaves from some distantly-remembered Red Cross issue.

"At least it'll warm your hands!" Jim Mackay would say, clutching his Klim-tin mug.

94

CHAPTER 14   P.G.70 AT MONTE URANO

Mercifully, with the still, cold days of Advent came a sprinkling of Food Parcels, extending our cuisine to porridge, oat-cakes, milk puddings and meat-and-vegetable stew commonly known as "M. 'n V."

Then the smoke-layer above the brew-patch was more substantial, long-time hovering protectively about our heads . . .

No man was more worthy of his double-loaf than Jim. He worked all day sometimes, shaving scores upon scores of fellow-prisoners with incredible speed and dexterity, keeping up non-stop his cheerful patter. He did as much as anybody to maintain the morale of the camp.

"Keep on lathering up," he'd advise the customer next-in-line, "The secret of a good shave is in the lathering, y'knaw!"

On the intervening days this wizard of the scissors cut our hair. The results were first-class.

Even in the spring of 1943, when the camp shop had been established and safety-razors could be bought, Jim was much in demand for shaving.

Before Christmas there was little we could buy except notebooks and pencils. However, consignments of locally-grown onions came in to help us through an exceptionally hungry three weeks. Pooling our money, Hal and I were able to buy three or four onions a week. With our knife, made from Red Cross tins, we diced these and simmered them in a flat oblong biscuit-tin.

The resulting soup tasted all-the-more delicious because for several days it was the only food we had! . . .

We did battle ceaselessly against vermin. Fleas abounded as at Bari, but their torment was as nothing compared with infestation by body-lice which fastened to our flesh, thrived on our blood and dwelt in our clothing. Men would sit semi-or-completely naked, meticulously examining every seam of their clothing. Smokers used glowing cigarette-ends, non-smokers their thumb-nails pincer-fashion, so that in the course of a morning about half a million would be executed. The next morning, if not before, we had to repeat the process. Indeed, at any time if one looked closely enough, a few lice were sure to be found! Some were so minute that they looked like stitches in the hem . . .

The Crew – June 1942

The Crew left to right:

Sgt Ken de Souza,	Sgt Taffy Coles,	Alf Frampton,	Hal Curtois,	Bert Bullock
Navigator	W/Op	F/Gunner	Pilot	R/Gunner

PG71 POW Camp Fayre. Thanks to Red Cross Food Parcels. Drumming up interest in starting Camp Newspaper ("70 Times")

"70 Times" the Padres and Medical Officers

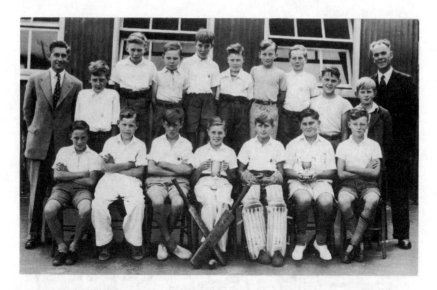

The Cowshed at Poole seen in background to team photo. Poole cricket champions. Mr W.H. Foote, Headmaster is standing right. Author standing left.

Italian POW's at Camp 63, in Scotland. Giovanni Brugnoni 3rd from the left, top row, hand on shoulder of man in front

GENERAL

SPORT

ENTERTAINMENT

Repatriate Writes from M.E.

A civilian England-to-Australia airgraph service has now been introduced. Cost, 8d. per airgraph.

Durham miners have this year had a week's holiday with pay, their first since war began.

Some agricultural "then and now" prices: A hen and 12 chickens, pre-war valuation 12/-, now fetch 30/-; 4 acres of cherry orchard ... about £500 pre-war; is now worth £5,050; 48 fat hens, selling pre-war at 3/8 a head, brought in £35.

A letter posted in Philadelphia, U.S.A. on April 27th, marked Breatland on June 16th was directed back here, and arrived on August 8th.

Princess Mary of Gloucester is to marry King Peter of Jugo-Slavia.

Bovasca (Yorks) Wings for Victory Week aimed at £125,000, got £143,500.

A mother writes claiming to have recognised her son in a photo taken at P.G.70 and published in a Red Cross bulletin. So it looks as though they've got us taped alright, boys.

And a recent P.O.W. repatriated after 2 years captivity, presumably writes that his own girl has since married, very little blamed.

Apropos of drink, we hope the beer's strong, but slightest hint is that 10th a pint is correct.

But (sorry, lads) we also learn that demobbed men will receive their credits by instalments, not in a lump sum.

"Digging for Victory" is still popular. In many London gardens strawberries, tomatoes and cherries are being grown.

No more civilian shoes can be sent in ZPt, says Red Cross. Only regulation Army boots are now allowed.

World mile record is now held by Gundahrig of Sweden, whose 4 mins. 6.2 secs. beats Wooderson's time by ¼ sec. The champion has also beaten previous 2 mile, 3 mile, 1500, 3000 and 5000 metres records.

At Brighton Cpl. Syd. Wooderson clocked 2 mins. 7.8 secs. for the half-mile; course was subsequently found to be about 30 yards over distance.

This year's Derby was won by Gordon Richards, with Harry Graves second and Cliff Richards third.

NEWS FROM SOMEWHERE

Belatedly, "all the winners" of the soccer season: Northern Cup Blackpool; Southern Cup Arsenal; Western League Swansea; Scottish League, Rangers; N.E. Scottish, Aberdeen; Northern League Orange, Liverpool; Southern League, Arsenal; Combined Counties Cup, Sunderland.

Now to cricket. Sgt. Maurice Leyland, batting for an Army XI against a Civil Defence team, knocked up 93. Civil Defence won the match by 4 wickets taking 158 (Gimblett 18), Rees 9 not out); Army 252 for 8 (declared) batting first.

Many of Canada's cricketers are bowling out for track labour ... Constructive of giving grant seen in the Lancashire Ladies' Len Hutton, knocked out of this Army ... after a series of P.T. is now playing for Pudsey St. L.'s in the Bradford League.

In the ring, Len Harvey is due to see his brother Kid Tomkins (9st), and Jim Brady (8-4) over distances.

Jack London, it is reported, beat Alf. Robinson in a Ground contest, but lacked the backing to stage a fight with Freddie Mills. Robinson is therefore meeting Mills for the British heavyweight title.

We hear that Benny Lynch was sparring partner to Pattinson for his title fight with Peter Kane.

Judy Garland is appearing on the London Stage. Among others who have graced the Atlantic is entertainer American troops in Blighty are Ginger Rogers, Kay Francis, Claudette Colbert and Ronald Colman.

For some time there has been an artificial shortage of films, new pictures being held back to boost up the value of re-issues, which now amount to about 50% of films exhibited.

New flicks now showing include: M.G.M.'s "Presenting Lily Mars", with Judy Garland and Gene Kelly, "Edge of Darkness" (Warner Bros.) starring Errol Flynn and Ann Sheridan. "Background to Danger" with George Raft and Brenda Marshall. Fox contribute "Hello Frisco, Hello", with John Payne, Alice Faye, Jack Oakie, and "Crash Dive", starring Tyrone Power. Paramount pictures include "China", with Alan Ladd, who is also featured in "Lucky Jordan". "Miss London Ltd." with Arthur Askey and Evelyn Dall, comes from G.F.D. Bob Hope and Dorothy Lamour lead in Radio's "They Got Me Covered", and "Flight for Freedom", with Rosalind Russell, is from the same studios.

Entire proceeds of "For Ever ... and a Day" are to go to Red Cross Stars, who gave their services free; include Anna Neagle, Merle Oberon, Ray Milland, Charles Laughton, Sir Cedric Hardwicke, Herbert Marshall, Robert Cummings, Ida Lupino, Victor McLaglen.

Joan Barry sues Charlie Chaplin 4,000 dollars a month for upkeep of illegitimate child. And that great big world keeps turning.

In celebration of Vaughan Williams' 70th birthday, the B.B.C. broadcast a weekly series of musical programmes of his works.

Master of the King's Musick is now Arnold Bax.

Among relics unearthed in screen revivals are Charlie Chaplin's one-time big hit, "The Gold Rush" and "Blood and Sand", featuring that oh-so-silent glamour boy Rudolph Valentino. West End stage revivals include "The Bells of New York" and "Sally".

Real Flash: Chaplin, now 55, has married 4th wife Oona O'Neill.

Repatriated from P.G.70 in May, Sgt. Jack PRIESTLEY, well-known of a Camp dramatic producer, sends a letter dated June 8th, 1943, which is of such interest that we quote liberally:

"Things you will already have 'the news flash' we have safely arrived in the Middle East. We were given a marvellous reception. I'm all over whether it were wiser to appease your curiosity or retain from making you homesick. When we arrived on board the Kaler we were waiting for us with English bags and a few minutes later we were given comfort bags from the Midland Red Cross containing razor, soap, towel, tooth-brush, tooth-paste, comb, mirror, pyjamas, handkerchiefs, even flowers — perhaps I've overlooked one or two items. Well we ruined our appetite sweetling ... sweets going down to soup, wheat beef, potatoes, veg., pudding and tea. Arriving back in the ward we found dried fruit from the Red Crescent. We managed to find time for tea, bread and fine bikers supper. Beer is rather limited and spirits expensive.

"We had a grand trip and when we arrived in this country got another reception. We were given another gift from the Red Cross ... this time containing 60 cigs., a copy of 'Gen', sweets etc. And again carried to either eating or drinking (Canadian beer) all the journey. The ambulances brought us here and we called — after another cup of tea. You might think by that time we'd be ready to give the stomach a rest, but I was able at 7 a.m. for my porridge, bacon, two eggs, tea, bread (for which) and (after we ever seen) butter and marmalade. The food is excellent of every single meal and I haven't even had indigestion.

"We're acclimatising bit gradually and I wondered when I visualise my next trip with this lot after the oh-so door of a few hurricanes. The smell — indeed R.D. and plenty of starch and some are grey skies. They are a bit higher but I haven't found anything I couldn't get.

"It has been to the flicks twice. Saw '45th Parallel' last night and am hoping to go to an E.N.S.A. revue on Friday. Well visiting yesterday, shopping at the E.F.I. this morning for foot polish, frame etc. I wish I could send you an interior snap.

"I'll write as often as possible. Regards to all, 'Jack'."

The above receives confirmation in a further letter from Pte. T. JOHNSTONE, posted in the Middle East on June 16th. Pte. JOHNSTONE describes how his party arrived after a cheerio voyage, the exchange of pleasantries taking place there. After commenting on a Scottish Red Cross gift they afterwards down to brass tacks. They already described by Sgt. PRIESTLEY.

He also bears out them ... and all were received in a billet ... over a night.

Pte. JOHNSTONE has already had several M.E. nights and 'no guy'. He says it has now been published in orders that all repatriated men are to return to Blighty.

''70 Times'' News from Home page

Giovanni Brugnoni and his wife, Ida

Crashed Blackburn Botha on golf course near Bobbington Airfield (now Halfpenny
Green) 29th June, 1941

The Brugnoni's farmstead, Monte Urano

The Cattle-shed (Oxen) at Monte Urano

Navigation Course Passing-out Group 3 A.O.S, Bobbington. Anson in background.
The author is third from the left sitting

Gino and Stella Brugnoni

The Brugnoni Family 1942

CHAPTER 15

Red Cross to the rescue

Thanks to the Red Cross some books arrived and at given times, weather permitting, a library-table was set up in front of the Central Hall. Censorship was strict and, like the bibles, all book-covers were scarred with diagonal slashes. Our literary diet consisted mainly of Tauschnitz editions, almost everything else being unacceptable to the Fascists. Still, it was a joy to be reading again.

One day a number of us were browsing at the book-table when we were disturbed by the rattle of the main gate being opened. Looking up, we beheld, not a new intake of prisoners, not Colonello Papa on one of his visits, not even the garbage truck coming in, but an Italian priest on a bicycle. He was of ample figure, his vestments precariously long for cycling, his shovel-hat apparently about to fall off his head at any moment.

When he passed close to us, tyres drumming on the weighbridge, we saw his round, smiling face. He chuckled at us, throwing up both his hands in a gesture that was a greeting, a blessing and nearly a catastrophe! Then he wobbled round the corner and out of sight.

That was my first introduction to Dom Mario.

By Christmas, with three compounds full, the camp strength topped the six-thousand mark. The enemy was transferring POWs from the more southerly camps such as Altamura and Bari.

From Bari at long last arrived Peter Davey to tell us that the camp down there was now empty; from Altamura came our RAF friend, Andy Arnot, whom I'd last seen in England. Navigators both, he and I had learnt our stars together at Harwell. A serious-minded Kirkcaldy Scot with twinkling pale blue eyes and merry bantering manner, he'd flown with 40 Squadron based at Shallufa, torpedo-carrying Wellingtons.

He was in Number 3 Compound in the company of hundreds of naval ratings. We took it in turns to visit each other, sometimes walking together round the "garden", objects of interest to the other POWs because, incredibly, we were the only three RAF people in the camp!

"D'ye ken we've taken Benghazi?" asked Andy.

"It's just a rumour," said Hal, "Don't believe all the rumours you hear in this place."

"No man, but it's a fact. We got it from Tenente Campanali."

Most pleasant of the Italian officers, the tenente used to stroll around the camp, officially keeping an eye on our activities. Either because he was out-of-sympathy with the Fascists or because he realised they were on the losing side, he took every opportunity to ingratiate himself with the British prisoners. From him we received up-to-date news of the Desert Rats' progress across North Africa.

"He was chatting to a couple of Navy lads in our compound and I happened to overhear," enlarged Andy. He had a nose for news, did Andy; he proved to be our champion eavesdropper!

At that moment, half-walking, half-running, Jim Mackay and John caught up with us.

"They're calling for the group leaders!" panted Jim.

"Yous gotter go 'n get the mail!" explained John . . .

That day in the last week in November Hal wrote exultantly in his diary:

"Received my first letter from Vi! Baby Rodney's walking now. Ken's had a letter too. Wonderful day!"

For me it was one of the most wonderful moments of my whole life. Even before I opened the letter, seeing my love's writing brought a lump to my throat. I had to climb up to my bunk to hide my tears, reading her letter over and over and over huddled under the blanket.

She was well and, a week before the arrival of my first letter, she'd been told that the Vatican radio had given out my name as a POW in Italy.

She also mentioned that the neighbour had been complaining about the weeds in our garden. However, she'd solved the problem by allowing an acquaintance to let his horse browse there. With war-work to be done, she had scarcely more opportunity for gardening than I had! Whether the neighbour preferred the horse to the weeds we never discovered.

Although the enemy had carried out his interrogation threat of not giving our names to the Red Cross, the news had got through. We suspected that our benefactor was Dom Mario.

Two weeks later I received a coloured photograph of Lillian — a beautiful picture, studio-produced.

"It's just as I remember her the day we met in Didcot!" commented Hal, admiring it.

Jim and John, Lofty and Bill said I was a lucky devil. Then Hal produced a bronze-coloured Red Cross biscuit-tin.

"I'll frame it for you," he said.

Such was Hal's dexterity that, within the hour the frame was finished and mounted on the bedpost. My love smiled out from an oval window of shining bronze. I was the envy of all who saw her . . .

As Red Cross Food Parcels began to filter through, the talents of our fellow-prisoners began to be revealed.

For example a POW in Number 3 Compound carved a beautiful crucifix which he set in the cover of Douglas Thompson's bible. That crucifix had originally been a POW spoon; the sculptor's tools nothing more than a nail-file and an assortment of stones!

Some of the musicians amongst us formed a mandolin band whose activities fluctuated with the arrival and non-arrival of Red Cross parcels. How the mandolins were procured we never knew: they were probably borrowed at the instigation of Dom Mario or Tenente Campanale or perhaps even Colonello Papa himself.

During Advent Hal and I tested our home-manufactured oven by making a Christmas cake. We spent hours preparing finely-grated breadcrumbs to use as flour to mix with Red-Cross fruit and butter. Baking was a lengthy process, the fuel being mostly wooden bed-slats. Like most POWs, by Christmas we had acquired the art of supporting our palliasses and ourselves on just three slats — "fore, aft and mizzen" as the Navy lads put it!

For icing our cake we used cocoa, milk powder and sugar. It was a hungry Advent — more like Lent really! — but we believed the sacrifices worthwhile. We were proud of our cake and our cooker.

Most beautiful of all was Bill Westaway's cake. White icing it had, exquisitely decorated, with the "Happy Christmas" message expertly written. We'd never seen better in a patissier's shop-window, yet the ingredients were limited to Red Cross Food Parcel contents; the tools of the trade nothing but his home-made tin-stove, his POW spoon and his POW bowl!

For a large number of us Christmas Day began with Holy Communion in an alcove of the Central Hall where Douglas Thompson had established altar and chapel. The chill of the early morning and the cold of the concrete floor only endowed with even deeper meaning the sharing of bread and wine. It was as though we were the first disciples at the first consecration.

Later we walked around the perimeter wishing each other "Happy Christmas", the sentinelli perched in their boxes above the rolls of barbed wire, awkward and bewildered like misplaced angels.

Came the Christmas-Day Service conducted by Douglas Thompson with the assistance of Peter Davey and Fred Hill and his accordeon. The only prisoners not thronging the "garden" were those unable to walk. The congregation must have numbered about five thousand. Could ever an act of worship have been more moving or more sincere? or hymns sung with more fervour? or prayers uttered with greater faith? or the message of a preacher given more heartening inspiration?

Douglas never prayed for a victory of arms — only for triumph over oppression and cruelty and intimidation. Even in those dark days we recognised these evils as incipient in ourselves and in our own nation: that they were now perpetrated by German Nazis, Italian Fascists and the Japanese army was a mere accident of History . . .

As we walked back to our Compound, Hal asked:

"Ken, what do you think about during the two-minute silence on Armistice Days?"

"The people who died or suffered in the Great War," I replied, surprised at his question.

He was silent a while. Then:

"But what was it all for — that Great War?"

His meaning began to dawn on me and I believe I gave the answer he was expecting.

"It was just a scrap between power-hungry nations."

"Then it wasn't worth it," he concluded, "I mean, not worth the sacrifice of millions of people."

He stopped opposite one of the sentry-boxes and lit a cigarette.

"You see, Ken, what bothers me is what the next generations are going to remember about this war."

"This war's different. We're defending our country against invasion by —."

"More than that," Hal interrupted, "We're fighting against thuggery in all its forms. But will they understand this? The best way of remembering us is to carry on our struggle for freedom."

At that moment the skilly-bugle sounded. We made our way towards the serving-point for Group 57 and Hal added:

"This must be one of the very few holy wars ever fought by Britain."

"Perhaps the only one!" I rejoined, watching our duty carriers struggle with the heavy tureen.

That Christmas Day it contained a good thick meaty nourishing stodge.

CHAPTER 16

The Seventy Times

Red Cross Food supplemented our Christmas fare and for our tea-party with Jim and John we supplied the slice of Christmas cake. The Geordies prepared a special brew of tea — all fresh tea-leaves!

We feasted well but wisely, reminded of the dangers of over-eating by the rumour that, following an hour's gluttony, a Compound-One POW was gravely ill in the Camp hospital.

In the evening a few prisoners in Number Three Compound began singing carols. It was not long before the singing was taken up by the rest of the six thousand men in P.G.70, Fred Hill keeping us going with his accordeon.

"Silent night, holy night
All is calm, all is bright
Sleep in Heavenly peace . . ."

I lay awake late that night thinking of my love and looking out through the window-spaces at the Christmas stars.

Hal's voice came up to me from the lower bunk: "Do you realise, Ken, exactly sixteen weeks ago we were in Bethlehem? That was a Friday too."

It seemed so very long ago, our four days' leave in Palestine — the truck-ride through orange groves to Tel-Aviv, the taxi-journey to Jerusalem and Bethlehem together with Bert and Alf, Bryn and Taffy: the precious moments in the stable-crypt of the Church of the Holy Nativity where candles would be burning still.

Then it had been back to the squadron for our Wellington to collect twenty-one holes over Tobruk the same night.

I whispered back:

"Sixteen weeks before that we were in England."

Immediately I'd said it. I regretted it, for Hal sighed deeply and I knew he was grieving for Vi and the children. I too felt a lump in my throat as memories of Christmasses with Lillian and our families overwhelmed me. However, I tried to cheer him:

"Don't worry! We'll make our escape before next Christmas"

"Goodnight. Ken!" retorted Hal abruptly, his tone rebuking my indiscretion in referring to "our escape". Even at that late hour someone could have been listening . . .

January and February were hungry months. Our numbers increased to over seven thousand as Number 4 Compound filled up, including our first Americans. Red Cross parcels arrived sporadically and in inadequate numbers, so that the relief they brought was very temporary.

The physical condition of men varied enormously, the fittest being the recently-captured Compound Four people: the weakest the old-stagers not receiving a double-loaf and foolish enough to sell food for cigarettes.

There was the contrast of those who strode energetically about the garden, and the poor devils too weak even to stand on their feet. For most of us during these long months escape had been impossible, not because of the barbed wire and the sentinelli, but simply because we were too weak from malnutrition.

However, with the coming of Spring and the snow at its most brilliant on those distant peaks, we began to hear talk of escape plans. It was a welcome change from the endless chatter about food and the spoon-by-spoon descriptions of recipes ad nauseam which had preoccupied POWs for so many weeks.

There was a tunnel scheme in which we were invited to join but declined because of the obvious lack of security. In the event, the Fascists waited until it was well-advanced then pounced and took the ring-leaders away for solitary confinement.

There were people who absconded from working parties, inevitably recaptured after one or two days' liberty. There was "Smithy" who had a penchant for secreting himself in unlikely places. Once it was under a pile of tins in the garbage truck. Another time he got himself locked in the Red Cross store where for two days he lived on chocolate pilfered from food parcels.

Some POWs were highly indignant at Smithy's pilfering. They were numbered among the anti-escape brigade which was very strong. Would-be escapers were told:

"You only risk your own lives and make things bad for the rest of us!"

But on the whole these nuisance escapes were excellent for morale. They agitated the guards and distressed Colonello Papa who was anxious that the Fascist hierarchy should receive good reports of his running of the camp. For the POWs they entailed some passing discomfort — solitary confinement for the would-be escapers, lengthy roll calls resented bitterly by the anti-escapers.

Sometime in May, when Food Parcels were coming in more regularly, Papa had loudspeakers mounted outside the central hall. After one "punishment roll call" which lasted about an hour and a half, we were treated to a long harangue about the folly of trying to escape.

"I am very sad when any prisoner try eescape. Eet ees bad for everybody and, understand, eescape ees eemposseebile! I look after you well, yes? and safe, yes? and one day you all go home. That is good, no?"

We thought it was very good — and rich!

The Colonello was courting the favour of both sides. A well-run, trouble-free camp would please the Fascists; a caring attitude towards the prisoners would be appreciated by the British.

The news had come in that the Allies were in control of North Africa from Egypt to Tunisia, and there were frightening rumours of an impending invasion of Sicily. Colonello Papa was having his first doubts about the Axis winning the war. It was wise to hedge one's bets! . . .

To this end, from time to time, he allowed us to hear a little music. It was especially diverting when the record was cracked and the loudspeakers crackling!

A more positive effort to improve our lot was the construction of the water-tower. In late spring some soldati arrived with long-handled spades to dig out the foundations. Then during roll call one morning an old lorry chugged in bearing bricks and the building began.

"It will be better for your washing and cleaning your utensils," Papa informed us.

They worked all day and every day except when it rained and, in late Summer when Sicily was firmly in Allied hands, the thing was finished — a remarkable gesture of goodwill!

Only the water dribbled and dripped as before.

"It will be very good, you will see," drooled the sugary loudspeaker voice, "It needs a leetle adjustment in the pipe!"

This was followed by a merry burst of "La donna è mobile" which served as a timely reminder of the fickleness of Lady Fortune.

Between Spring and Summer, as feeding became adequate, our lives were remarkably transformed. Malnutrition was banished and our returning energy found expression in all kinds of activities — talks; classes, albeit without books; clubs, albeit without equipment; football, rugger and morning P.T.; in the central hall the creation of a theatre, and on the walls outside the posting of the sheets of the wall newspaper.

Furthermore, thanks to a steady influx of Red Cross medical supplies and to Major Parkes' persuasive powers with Colonello Papa, the Camp Hospital was properly established. It was a great achievement.

One day in early March at skilly-time, after the carriers had taken away the tureens, there was an unusually large number of cadgers of embers outside the cookhouse. As each was carrying his brew-stove, space was very limited.

Nobody quite knew how it happened, but a POW who was walking by at the time somehow stumbled and fell against the trip-wire. Came a yell from the sentry box above and the click of a rifle.

He was just picking himself up when the trigger was squeezed.

Crack! One solitary shot! It echoed in the four compounds. We all stopped feeding and looked at each other in alarm.

Our alarm was justified for the aim had been good. Through the open doors of No. 2 Compound we saw the soldati bearing away the lifeless body.

It was a sharp reminder that, although material conditions were improving, we were still subject to the enemy's code of warfare and Death was always lurking round the corner . . .

That night, too, I lay awake. No stars were to be seen through the window-spaces. The only light to penetrate the blackness was the enemy searchlight remorselessly sweeping the outside area.

"No good anyone trying to get away over the wire!" I whispered to Hal.

But he was already far away, breathing deeply and rhythmically, probably dreaming of his home in Pinner . . .

After the trip-wire tragedy, life in P.G.70 carried on as before, only becoming richer and more varied. We had an Auto Club without automobiles, a Cycling Club without bicycles, a Transport Club with no other transport than Shanks's Pony. On the other hand, the Chess Club possessed home-made chess sets; the French Club was run by a qualified French teacher, and the Insurance Circle was staffed by experts, one of them Hal. As for the Church in its various denominations, a church tent was erected in the garden.

The most remarkable achievement of all was the Camp Theatre in the central hall. Stage sets were constructed from Red Cross crates and the painting of the scenery depended on two basic colour sources — crushed mepacrin anti-malaria tablets (yellow) and Italian substitute coffee which tasted like burnt acorns but made good brown paint, light or dark according to its concentration.

Producer Fred Hindle was ambitious from the start. That he was right to be so was proved by one of the first productions, "The Desert Song". We unearthed first-class musical talent, costumes were excellent and, most impressive of all, four men with a flair for assuming female roles.

These stage "women" were so real that they had a stunning effect on POWs deprived of female company for a year or more.

Ambition begot ambition and in August Frank Lazarre produced "Philadelphia Story". Thanks to the ingenuity of the wardrobe master and his costumiers the dressing was always superb.

If life in POW camps were to be judged solely from those better days, then it could be comparable to that of an overcrowded holiday camp which had somehow got infested with fleas and body-lice. But it should never be forgotten that the better days only came to pass by courtesy of the Red Cross.

Now at P.G.70 Colonello Papa encouraged all the new-found activities. With the Allies already in control in Sicily he had very good reason! . . .

"We won't have any need to escape after all," declared Hal, "We'll soon be liberated!"

"Now who's the optimist?" I chided, adding, "I don't yet know how we're going to get out of the camp, but, when we do, we mustn't get picked up just because we look English . . ."

"Good Heavens, man, ye'll never look English" interrupted a Scotch voice. We hadn't realised that Andy Arnot was walking close behind us. "And what's all this drivel about escape?"

"It's Ken's obsession," Hal explained, "He won't have it that were about to be liberated."

"I'm not too sure about that either. Maybe we won't invade Italy at all, and I dinna fancy having two guid pals shot trying to escape!"

"We won't do anything rash," I promised, "but there's no harm in some preliminary planning. For example, I've been watching the Italians working on the water-tower. They walk like this." I performed a mime to demonstrate their slouch. "And when they beckon their mates they wave their arms like this."

Andy and Hal were splitting their sides.

"Ye look Italian reet enough!" laughed Andy.

"For comic opera!" added Hal.

"I'll be better with practice," I assured them,

"The point is, if we do ever get out of the camp, at least one of us must look like an Italian of the district."

"Aye, but can you speak the lingo?"

"Poco, poco, ma sto imperando. I'm learning from Hal's book."

One day Hal had produced a slim booklet which formed part of Hugo's Italian course. I'd been studying it assiduously.

"I thought you amused yourself writing stories," said Andy.

"I've written a story about a Grimsby skipper,"I acknowledged, "I don't know whether it's any good but Tenente Caporale thinks it is."

"Tenente Caporale! He'll be no judge. His knowledge of English is not what you'd call extensive."

"Extensive enough to translate my story!" Both Hal and Andy looked puzzled and I continued:

"I've got official permission to go through to the admin. offices to use the typewriter. That's where I was this morning, bashing away at the Olivetti and taking a look at the lie of the land through the open window. I could have walked out easily. Between the offices and the road there's only a low wall and a single strand of wire."

We walked on round the perimeter in silence after that . . .

Later that night Hal asked,

"Ken do you really think we could escape through the admin. offices?"

"I don't know. But for the time being it's a useful observation point. The main thing is for us to be prepared."

The next day I asked the tenente if the Commandant would favour the establishment of a camp newspaper. I had the idea of typing the stencils and getting them duplicated. The response was so enthusiastic that I even suggested the possibility of getting it properly printed. So great was his anxiety to please that he promised to make enquiries about this.

I thought that if typing were decided upon, other POWs might be allowed into the Admin. office to help out with typing and duplicating. Thence proceeded various escape possibilities.

Later the same week the Camp Fayre took place. I had a pitch in the garden allocated to the "Camp Newspaper" where with serio-comic market-trader patter, I sought to interest the P.G.70 public in the idea. I also wore in my forage cap a label bearing the intended title: "THE PINNACLE". This referred to Colonello Papa's water-tower which now dominated the camp.

One of the features which I was advertising was a "News from Home" column. With the active co-operation of the eight-thousand men a lot of interesting, uncensorable news could be gathered from the incoming mail. And perhaps, among so many letters, an occasional item which the censor had missed!

The other object of my campaign was to get together the people interested in writing and producing the paper. This was handsomely achieved for the next day Eric Hurst from Number 4 Compound came across for a chat. Eric was by profession a journalist.

"That was a useful bit of advertising. The camp's really interested now. The only drawback to a printed or cyclostyled newspaper is that it may take time to get it organised and it also makes us dependent on the Italians for supplies — reams of paper, for example."

I agreed, delighted to have found somebody of Eric's calibre. He went on:

"I've already made some enquiries about a Wall Newspaper to be posted outside the central hall. I've got together the artists on the camp. They'd do all the printing and illustrations. I think we'd be allowed the use of the weighing room as our editorial office and we could probably get supplies from Papa. What d'you think, Ken?"

I thought it was excellent because we could make a start almost immediately.

"We have already voted to call it 'The Seventy Times'. But if you feel strongly about 'The Pinnacle' —."

" 'The Seventy Times' it is!" I consented happily.

Ten days later the first issue of "The Seventy Times" appeared. Affixed to the wall outside the central hall were ten large news-sheets, about 26″ ✕ 18″ in size, meticulously hand-printed and beautifully illustrated. Display and maintenance was the task of Dave Fogden who so arranged the spacing that up to five people could comfortably gather at each page, thus accommodating fifty readers at any given time.

Production of the four-column news pages, and indeed the art and cartoon pages was the remarkable achievement of the Art Staff, Messrs. Adams, Campbell, George, Green, Newell and White. They managed it, working in cramped conditions in what was once the weighing-scales room. Their desks were Red Cross crates: their materials pens, brushes and Indian ink.

Peter Grant who had been working with me on the "Pinnacle" project, came in as reporter. Our "News from Somewhere" page told of the exploits of Sweden's Gundaheig in running the mile in 4 minutes 6.2 seconds, of Corporal Sydney Wooderson's fast half mile at Brighton: of Sergeant Maurice Leyland knocking up 93 runs for An Army XI, and of Liverpool winning the Football Northern League, Arsenal the Southern League and Cup, the Northern Cup going to Blackpool. We recorded that Judy Garland was appearing on the London stage and that the films currently showing in England included Warner Bros' "Edge of Darkness" starring Errol Flynn and Anne Sheridan, and "Background to Danger" with George Raft and Brenda Marshall.

The page aroused considerable interest and forged another link with Home.

The day after the third issue appeared, Dom Mario pedalled into the camp, camera slung over his shoulder. We didn't know until then that he was an expert photographer. He leaned his bicycle against the wall where it would not interfere with the reading public and set to work in the manner of a professional. He checked the lightmeter, the distances and the settings. Then he carefully photographed each page of "The Seventy Times", one after the other, moving methodically along the line.

The Appenines shed their last patches of snow as throughout July and August the news of the war continued to improve. Then suddenly the whole camp was agog. Hal wrote in his diary:

"Sunday, 5th September. Received news that the Allies have landed in Reggio Calabria. Expect to be liberated any day now."

Rumour was rife. Lofty had reliable information that paratroops had landed not far away; John reckoned that the enemy wouldn't stretch their resources by trying to defend this part of Italy; Bill Westaway thought liberation was at hand while Hal had the air of a successful prophet. Only Andy, the canny Scot, sounded the note of caution:

"It's one thing to set foot in the toe of Italy. It's quite another to advance up into the boot proper. There's an awful lot of mountainous country and rivers to cross. Ye can be sure they'll have bridges to repair, road blocks to clear and all the rest."

But he was in the minority. The Allies could land anywhere along the coast, he was told, not to mention paratroops being put down to hold key positions. The idea of an Army slogging it out advancing along a "line" was outmoded. Modern warfare was fluid, one created pockets of resistance behind the enemy, etc., etc.

We watched the skies for Allied aircraft, but all in vain. The skies here were strangely quiet. On the morning of Wednesday, 8th September a Junkers 52 plodded southward, its three engines chugging laboriously. We imagined it packed with reinforcement German troops.

For a long time the skilly-bugle had been superseded by the skilly-bagpipes as we now had many Highlanders in our midst. It was a heartening sound which did much for our morale.

Those pipes had a specially triumphant sound that day and when the groups met at the tureens there was a cacaphony of excited chatter such as had never been heard before in P.G.70.

We awoke the next morning to the sight of unmanned sentry-boxes. The Italian guards had departed during the night.

Then over the loudspeaker, Warrant-Officer Atkinson requested us to line up in our groups as for a roll-call. No sooner said than done. Speaking on behalf of Major Parkes, the senior officer, he announced:

"Yesterday at 1800 hours the Italians signed an Armistice."

CHAPTER 17

Dixies — with lids

Our cheering must surely have been heard for miles around. When at long last it subsided, Atkinson continued:

"We have received orders from Allied High Command. We are to stay put in the camp and await the arrival of our troops."

For a couple of days Hal, like most of the other POWs, lived in expectation of immediate liberation vainly searching land and sky for signs of the Allied presence.

As for me, I was under treatment in the camp hospital. A hole had opened up in my right ankle and was suppurating profusely.

"Clean him up and I'll look at him again this evening," said Major Parkes.

I was overjoyed to discover that the medical orderly was none other than Canadian Sam. He had stayed on in Benghazi until the first days of November when the camp was cleared.

"I reckon this trouble comes from the time you scraped your knees in the desert," he declared as he bathed the ankle in hot water, adding, "Anyway, you'll mend!"

Just then Fred Hill began playing his accordeon. It wasn't a hymn, he was only trying to cheer us, but when Sam departed I thankfully covered my ears with the bed-clothes.

"Wotcher Ken! Them knees again, is it"

I looked up. Standing beside my bed was the wounded Bert whom I'd last seen in the hospital tent at Benghazi.

I explained my trivial case and turned the question back to him.

"I'm O.K. now, thanks," he replied, "Just a bit o' shrapnel left in there, see. Get it taken out in Blighty maybe."

"How about your mate Jack?"

"Didn't you hear? Doc Parkes got him repatriated. One of the first to go, he was. He's got to have that leg amputated."

During the days of hunger and misery there had been no question of repatriation. But now the Red Cross had found us and the tide of war had turned against the thugs. The worst hospital cases were being sent home . . .

Bert just had time to tell me that he had been moved to P.G.70 six weeks previously and that he was in No. 4 Compound before Fred Hill arrived at the foot of my bed.

"Join in if you know the words, fellers," he encouraged us and fortissimo launched into "He who would valiant be." . . .

Later I was able to speak with Reverend Peter Davey who visited the hospital regularly. Strange that in all the time since Bari, we'd never had any conversation. He was an extremely busy man who did so much for so many in his unassuming way.

Returning as promised, Major Parkes prescribed a sulfonamide-powder dusting for my ankle.

"You can leave hospital in the morning," he told me, "Then stay out in the open air as much as possible and let the sun get at it." . . .

During that same night, silently and undetected, the troops arrived to take over P.G.70.

When I limped back into the camp. I saw them, nonchalant in the sentry-boxes, machine-guns mounted, immaculate in their grey uniforms — soldiers of the Third Reich.

Never did jubilation change so quickly to black despair! Where was the Allied Army? Had the invasion failed? Or perhaps we'd been told a pack of lies and it had never taken place:

"To think we could have walked out yesterday with no one to stop us!" muttered Hal gloomily.

"What! All of us!" I exclaimed, "Eight thousand unarmed men roaming the countryside. It would have meant disaster — especially if the S.S. had decided to take a hand!"

Hal sighed deeply and lit a cigarette. The Germans had already organised a liberal cigarette issue.

"Surely Ken, you've heard the news? They're going to move us to Austria. I don't see how we're ever going to escape!"

Now that the Italians were gone I could no longer go through to the admin. offices. Making our exit over the low wall at the front was no longer a possibility.

I hid my own despondency and tried to cheer him up.

At least the treatment we received from the Germans was better than anything we'd encountered previously. Food and cigarettes were plentiful, and the attitude of our guards was strangely friendly.

"Treat the sheep well and they'll go willingly to the slaughter!" observed Jim Mackay while John added darkly, "It'll be different when we get to the Stalags!"

After an ample lunch I made my way to the Editorial Office of "The Seventy Times" — the weighing-room where, prior to the war, the weights of the flax-carts were recorded. The scale-fitting had long since been removed.

When I arrived, Eric Hurst and the rest of the staff were busy taking away Red Cross crates, artists materials, paper and all evidence that the room had recently been used.

At last, the office being empty of all furnishing, we stood about awkwardly, sad at the ending of a unique and successful project.

CHAPTER 17   DIXIES — WITH LIDS

Eric was idly toying with his skilly-spoon.

Presently he cleared his throat in an embarrassed manner and addressed me. All eyes then turned on me and I had the impression that they must have been talking about me previously.

"Ken, we've got a proposition to put to you. We don't know how you'll take it, but whatever you do, we shall respect your decision."

I nodded encouragingly and he explained:

"You've probably noticed that, although we have six on the Art Staff, there have seldom been more than four working at any given time."

"The office is too small for six people," I commented, "It was a good idea to work a shift system."

"I suppose it was a shift system of sorts, Adams and Campbell, George and Green, Newell and White — three pairs. Now come and see what the off-duty pair were doing most of their time."

So saying he bent down and, using the handle of his spoon, levered up the end of a loose floor-board. Newell and White stooped to help him while the other four lounged in front of the window.

With two short lengths of floorboard removed I could see the shaft which had once linked the scales to the weighbridge.

"We didn't cut these boards," said Newell. "It must be the way they got down to service the mechanism."

"Go on down, Ken, and have a look," invited Campbell.

Once I'd let myself down into the hole they replaced the boards, I crawled through the tunnel which was no more than ten or twelve feet long.

As I entered the cavity below the weighbridge, I was surprised at the amount of light filtering in at the edges of the platform. But what surprised me most of all was the evidence of the hard work put in by my "Seventy Times" colleagues. How many days or weeks it had taken them I would never know, only that down there below the steel girders they had built, side by side, two wooden-slatted beds. They had also smuggled in a palliasse and blanket for each.

The oblong cavity formed a three-foot high concrete-sided cell approximately eight-foot by four-foot in area. The tops of the walls were flanged to allow for the movement of the steel platform. This also admitted enough air to make life tolerable for anybody taking up residence below.

It was also perfectly dry down there as was to be expected at the end of a hot Italian summer. I lay back on one of the beds studying the underside of the platform. It was in good condition with no sign of rust.

I was startled as footsteps suddenly thundered across it. It trembled under the weight of three or four people as did the assembly of girders below it. But the moving parts must have been well-lubricated for I detected no creaks or squeaks.

I wriggled back to the weighing office, pushed open the two floor-boards and climbed out.

"A most comfortable hiding-place!" I congratulated them.

"Glad you think so, Ken," rejoined Eric, "because in all fairness we're offering it to you as a possible means of escape —"

"Don't be a bloody fool, Ken!" interrupted Campbell.

"It'd be suicide to try it on the Germans!" Adams exclaimed.

The other four all nodded their agreement.

"If the Fascists had had the job of moving us out of the camp, two of us would have tried it."

"We reckon the German search will be more thorough, and they'll probably shoot anyone they find!" said Newell.

" 'Shot trying to escape' — a pathetic epitaph!" put in Green.

"They'll probably lob a few grenades around anyway!" added Grant.

Eric concluded:

"As you see, Ken, we're not very optimistic, but it's up to you to make your own decision."

For me the decision was already made but I had first to consult Hal.

"I'll let you know within half-an-hour," replied, adding, "And thanks!" . . .

I was glad to find Hal on his own. He was sitting under a tree reading.

"Come on, Ken. Sit down and get the sun on your ankle."

I did so and, lowering my voice, told him about the weighbridge hide-out and the escape-scheme that had formed in my mind.

"Given a couple of Red-Cross parcels and a supply of water, you and I could live down there for at least three weeks — certainly until long after the Germans have emptied the camp."

"How can we lay in a supply of water?" Hal prompted me with the obvious question.

I explained:

"They plan to move out Number 1 Compound POWs tomorrow or the next day. There are bound to be some large cooking-pots or dixies left behind in the cookhouse. If we put two of those under the platform, one can serve as the water-container, the other as our latrine."

"With lids!" declared Hal, smiling at last.

"With lids," I agreed.

Hal closed his book and stood up.

"Let's take a turn round the perimeter," he suggested.

We walked awhile in silence. Then Hal observed:

"Because it's in a central position, the weighbridge is as far away from any of the sentry-boxes as you could get. If we did just happen to snore or cough or sneeze, it's unlikely that anyone would hear."

"Hal, I don't suppose the sentry-boxes will be manned once the camp has been cleared of prisoners."

"We don't know for sure. But I was thinking of the time before all our mates have been moved out. At dead of night we don't want some German to hear a fruity snore rising up from below the ground."

"A good point!" I laughed, "Therefore we mustn't both sleep at the same time."

"Right! Then we'll have a rota system." He paused to light another cigarette. After a moment's reflection he spoke briskly — the old Hal, the man of action I knew so well.

"I'll see Atkinson. He's the only person we'll tell and he'll let us have a couple of Red Cross parcels for sure."

"Don't you think Andy should be in the know?" I protested, regretting that there wasn't room for three underneath the platform.

"Not even Andy," persisted Hal.

"There's no one more trustworthy!" I objected.

"True enough, but someone's bound to ask him where we are. That means he'll have to make up some story or other. Safest to tell no one except the Camp Leader."

I hurried back to the central hall to inform Eric and the others of our decision . . .

Next morning the exodus began. Group by Group the two thousand POW's of Compound One, some carrying their "Smoky-Joes", were marched away escorted by grim-faced German guards.

"Down to the railway station for another bloody excursion!" observed Lofty, "Our turn next, Ken." Choked by the bitter disillusion of the moment and unable to explain that Hal and I were about to lay our lives on the line to avoid that fate, I clapped Lofty on the shoulder and walked away. At the same time I glimpsed Hal deep in conversation with Warrant-Officer Atkinson.

Down at the far end of the perimeter I found Newell and White studying the rear barbed-wire gate. It was the way working-parties used to come and go.

"This would be the easiest place to get through —" White was saying.

"I've come for help!" I butted in, then immediately regretted my rudeness.

"Shoot!" encouraged Newell.

"Just to carry a dixie from the Compound One cookhouse — Please!"

"When?" White spoke as if his day was crammed with important appointments.

"Come along over when you hear the bagpipes."

"Done!" agreed Newell, "See you there!"

I left the two of them chatting and returned across the "garden". As I reached the place where the church tent had once stood, the tall gate was closing behind the last of Compound One POW's. I heard the metallic clatter as it was slammed shut.

Then I strolled round to Compound One cookhouse which like the other cookhouses contained a row of brick fireplaces and at one end a tap from which water could regularly be persuaded to flow. Also like the other cookhouses it was completely open on one side. This made the carriers' job easier for by the time the pipes sounded, the cooks had lined up several filled

113

dixies along the length of the floor. No need to queue or jockey for position in a doorway: it was simply up carrying-poles and away.

I noted with relief the empty dixies and poles neatly stacked in one corner.

Then turning away I came near that part of the trip-wire where the Italian sentry had shot a man dead. The boyish-looking German above me now, apparently oblivious to my presence, was munching a sausage . . .

An hour or so later the bagpipes sounded a lament for the departed and for those still to depart. Hal and I found the same youngster on sentry-duty, still chewing, still quite disinterested.

Out of the corner of his eye, he doubtless saw us filling a dixie at the tap, saw Newell and White carry away an empty dixie but could have had no inkling that this activity has anything to do with an escape attempt.

Likewise a few minutes later other sentries would have noticed the group of prisoners in the little room near the weighbridge. Absurd to suppose they were stowing cookhouse dixies under the floor! . . .

CHAPTER 18

Below the Bridge

"Where the hell have you two been?" Lofty greeted me as he stirred the pot. "You nearly missed your skilly."

"Sorry mate," apologised Hal, "We've been tidying up the newspaper office." And we held forth our bowls for the scrapings at the bottom of the tureen . . .

During the late afternoon, when the incredible variety of "Smoky-Joes" were assembled on the brew-patch, we collected our two Red Cross parcels and deposited them on the girders under the weighbridge platform. We also put down there items of clothing such as Italian-issue foot-cloths, socks being a rarity; Hal's bulging satchel, books and cigarettes.

Thus we were ready to make our departure at a moment's notice with only small light articles to carry. Such as the biscuit-tin framed photo of Lillian still mounted on my bed in Number 2 Compound.

The last remark Jim Mackay made that night was:

"There's a strong rumour they're going to move out our compound the day after tomorrow."

Because he was Camp Hairdresser, moving around and talking to all and sundry, Jim's rumours were invariably true.

Next day, Sunday, 12th September, 1943, the Reverend Douglas Thompson held what was to be the last Religious Service in P.G.70.

Hal and I stood at the back of the huge congregation until prayers were said and Douglas announced the hymn:

"The Lord's my Shepherd."

Fred squeezed out the tune of Crimond on his accordeon; six thousand POWs sang with a fervour born of suffering and deprivation:

"The Lord's my Shepherd, I'll not want.

He makes me down to lie . . ."

The words rang in our ears and in our hearts as we locked the glass-panelled door of the weighing-office behind us; pocketed the key; descended into the tunnel, replacing the boards from underneath; finally wriggling through to our cell to lie ourselves down on the prepared beds.

Neither of us spoke. From afar we were still members of Douglas Thompson's congregation. When the hymn ended we strained our ears to hear his voice. It came to us strangely clear:

"The Lord bless you and keep you,

115

The Lord make His face to shine upon you. The Lord lift up the light of his countenance upon you,

And give you Peace.

Now and for evermore . . ."

I took the tin-framed photo of Lillian from my pocket and propped it up against the side of a steel girder . . .

Came a hubbub of voices followed by a deafening stampede across our roof. The prisoners were returning to their Compounds.

I did not see what Hal wrote in his diary. It cannot have been more than a few words for the light soon faded.

Forgetting all about our plans for a shift system, we lay our heads down to enjoy the sleep of men who had achieved what they'd set out to do . . .

I was awakened by a German voice close at hand shouting orders. Hal put his finger on his lips and pointed upwards. Whoever stood on the bridge began strutting to and fro — thump, thump, thump, thump, click, click! thump, thump, thump, thump, click, click! Four paces on the bridge, two paces off.

Soon we heard the murmur of voices and once again the thudding of many feet. The German rapped out another command. Voices and feet were instantly stilled. Then somewhere near the main gate Atkinson was talking but we couldn't make out his words: he seemed far away in another world.

The thudding started up again. It was a drum-roll which went on and on and on and we inside the drum put our hands over our ears until, after an immeasurable period of time, the footsteps stopped beating.

We knew that the first dozen groups would already have passed through the gate and the two of us sat up motionless, straining our ears to catch every last sound of our friends' departure. There were so many friends: not only Jim Mackay and his mate John, cheerful Fred Hill of the "Sally-Ann", Lofty Breadmore the humorist, the talented Westaway, but also hundreds of others who had suffered the hungry winter with us, who had in various ways helped us to endure . . .

After an age it came — the slamming of the gate and the ultimate silence . . .

That was Monday.

On Tuesday Compound Three POWs were moved out of the camp. That included Andy Arnot, and I grieved bitterly that he couldn't be escaping with us.

Wednesday was quiet with only Number Four Compound remaining, mostly recently-captured men including many Americans.

We spent most of the time reading, tilting our books where the daylight shafted in at the edges of the platform. From time to time, to my chagrin, Hal smoked a cigarette. I imagined tell-tale wisps of fragrant, blue smoke rising from the weighbridge. However, if there were, nobody took any notice.

We drank water or Klim milk in moderation, ate sparingly and our latrine-dixie came in for little use.

116

CHAPTER 18   BELOW THE BRIDGE

Thursday, 15th September was P.G.70's last day. As before, the German strutted above us, and having barked his orders, departed presumably for the main gate. For the last time we heard Warrant-Officer Atkinson's voice, then the cavalcade thundered by; receded, then at a command halted.

We waited breathlessly for the moment of departure. It did not come immediately.

Instead we heard footsteps running, doors being flung open, beds being overturned, and intermittently the strident voices of the enemy soldiers searching the camp. We dared neither move nor breathe. "Come on out, you British. Raus! Raus! We know you're in there!" We were startled by a volley of shots. They were searching the water-tower.

There were groups hunting everywhere. Shouting and bursts of automatic rifle-fire sounded in all the compounds.

Then came the moment that we had been dreading.

Heavy boots pounded the metal platform. Two or three enemy soldiers reached the central hall. "Come on out, you British!" The repeated command was loud in our ears.

As they entered the central hall they must have noticed the little room on their right. The door was rattled violently.

Instinctively Hal clutched his satchel containing the key. Someone tried the door again. A pause. A muttered conversation — presumably one man telling his mate the room was empty anyway. Easy to see that through the glass panel.

The search moved farther into the hall.

After an age the footsteps drew near again. Suddenly at the entrance they stopped.

We froze. Had they decided to investigate the weighbridge?

Came the click of a rifle, more bursts of automatic fire. They were spraying bullets around the hall.

Down below the platform the sound was deafening. We felt the whip of every shot.

The heavy-booted feet thudded overhead again, then scrunched away across the stony ground. Another command. A muttering and a shuffling which merged, as it faded, into the merest whisper. Faded and died.

We sat, keyed-up, waiting through the silence for the sound that was to come. After an age we heard it, distantly and for the last time, the metallic slam of the gate . . .

CHAPTER 19

*The Contadini

We had planned to reside under the weighbridge for a week at the very least before making our final exit through the wire. A more immediate attempt could have met with disaster: we reasoned that some Germans might remain awhile in the neighbourhood on the look-out for stray POWs.

Contrary to our expectations, that week proved to be one of the most uneventful of our lives.

On Friday, hearing no signs of activity whatsoever, we were sorely tempted to make our breakout there and then.

"No good making a plan if we don't stick to it!" declared Hal.

So we passed the hours reading; occasionally chatting in whispers; and much of the time sleeping, taking care that when one slept the other was always awake.

Perhaps because of the contrast in our characters, ours was an ideal partnership — the perfect point-and-counterpoint. We had no need of a formal rota and had the happy knack of fitting in with each other.

Saturday was the day sentries began patrolling from the main gate round the central hall and back again. At first we were startled by the rhythmic thud of boots on our roof — just four measured paces, returning at the end of four minutes.

Then we got to timing the sentries and trying to distinguish them by their tread. There seemed to be two, one slower and heavier than the other. When Slow was on duty the time interval varied from four minutes to six minutes. The other was meticulously punctual.

On Monday evening we heard the snarl of heavy trucks grinding, low-gear, down the hill. When they pulled into the camp for the night, we were able to count them as, one after the other they switched off their engines. There were three of them.

Early the following morning, soon after six o'clock by Hal's watch, they pulled out again.

The same thing happened the following three nights, but on Thursday night there was only one truck.

On Friday the camp was strangely quiet. There was no sign of the sentries nor did any more trucks arrive.

The next day towards one o'clock Hal climbed out. He waited awhile

* The peasant folk

119

before unlocking the weighing-room door, then tiptoed into the central hall to reconnoitre. There were windows on three sides but none at the far end of the hall. Thus he could only get an oblique view of the Admin. block area at the front; and only then by climbing onto one of the top bunks.

When he came back he was exhausted. He lay a few seconds recovering his breath.

"These thirteen days on the bed sure have weakened me!" he panted.

I nodded sympathetically.

"Did you see anyone, Hal?"

"Three Fascists out in the open having their lunch. They must have been Fascists because no other Italians would be wearing military uniform. But the camp itself is empty. Jerry left the hall in a hell of a mess — broken beds, palliasses and straw everywhere!"

The following three days we took it in turns to make sorties at various times. We gained much-needed exercise and also the valuable information that the guards lunched daily at one o'clock.

On the morning of Michaelmas a group of Italian peasant-women came into the camp. As I quickly rejoined Hal we heard them laughing and chattering as they entered the hall. Presently we heard the hiss of moving straw and we guessed they were emptying palliasses.

*"The contadine!" cried Hal, "Thank God!"

Never doubting the friendliness of the Italian peasants, I took the key from Hal and wriggled back through the tunnel.

When I opened the weighing-office door, I saw two black-clad young women thrusting a heap of straw into a large sack.

I remained still, wondering how I could make myself known without frightening them. Sudden screams would surely alert the Fascisti guards.

One of the women placed the sack of straw on her head and made her way through piles of rubbish across the hall. The other stayed to fill more sacks.

I approached and coughed to attract her attention. "Scusi!"

Completely engrossed in what she was doing, she didn't hear me at first. "Scusi signora! Per favore!"

She dropped her armful of straw, turned and faced me, her eyes wide with terror. I put my finger to my lips and said quickly:

"Non ha paura, signora. Sono prigionero inglese."

"O Mamma mia! Mamma mia!" she gasped. Then,

†"Da dov'è venuto?"

"Sono stato sotto la basculla."

She looked at me in disbelief but, despite my unkempt appearance, quickly overcame her fear. She gestured for me to wait where I was. Then without apparent haste she went on down the hall. Those moments of waiting were

* Contadine = peasant-women
† Where did you come from?

120

an eternity. I realised that two courses were open to her: she could bring other contadine to our aid; or, if fear of enemy reprisals got the upper hand, she could summon the Fascisti guards from the front of the camp.

I re-entered the weighing-office, knelt down and called through the tunnel.

"Hal, you can come out now. I think it's going to be all right!"

In my heart I prayed that it was all right. I believed in the peasant-woman — but one could never be certain.

Watching Hal emerge, haggard and unshaven, I realised what a frightening apparition I myself must have been. No wonder she had been terrified.

As we returned to the hall we saw a group of six contadine wading through the straw towards us. They were chattering excitedly.

When they reached us they stopped talking. The one to whom I had made myself known was obviously the elected spokeswoman.

*"Quanto tempo sotta la basculla — voi?" she demanded.

†"Diciasette giorni," I replied.

The spokeswoman glanced back towards the front of the camp and, lowering her voice, told me:

‡"Aspetti ancora un po' sotto la basculla. Ritorneremo a mezzogiorno."

Hal consulted his watch and she grabbed his wrist and pointed to the twelve:

"Ecco! Mezzogiorno!"

Then satisfied that we understood they'd be returning at midday, she introduced herself, "Io Maria," smiled encouragingly, and promptly departed with her five friends.

The time was nearly eleven o'clock, leaving us an hour in which to wash, shave and make ourselves presentable. No longer any need to economise with the water.

Shaving was painful, razors blunt and the water cold. We spent some minutes sticking tiny pieces of blocco-notto paper over our cuts.

We also packed our belongings into the two Red Cross cardboard boxes and into Hal's satchel to be ready to make a quick exit.

During the few minutes before midday we brought out our possessions, blankets and palliasses included, and laid them on the floor of the weighing-office.

Maria was true to her word. At twelve o'clock exactly she and her friends, carrying baskets on their heads, sauntered in through the back entrance. We noticed that the barbed-wire gate had already been left ajar.

Once in the hall they deposited their baskets on the floor. All were empty except Maria's which was heaped with grapes. She handed these to us.

††"Manya!" she invited.

We devoured the sweet juicy grapes with relish.

* How long have you been under the weighbridge?
† Seventeen days.
‡ Wait under the weighbridge a little while longer. We'll come back at midday.
†† Manya = Ascoli Piceno dialect for "mangia" = eat!

While we did so the women loaded cardboard boxes, blankets, satchel, rolled-up palliasses, our khaki pullovers and everything else into their baskets.

Immediately all was ready, Maria made that curious gesture which an English mind translates as "Go away!" but which in fact means "Come here!" or "Follow me!"

We followed her and her partner while the others disposed themselves around us, one either side and two behind.

In the same way as they had sauntered into the camp so they — and we! — sauntered out. Just once I glanced back towards where the Fascisti would be having lunch. I could not see them for they were hidden by the central hall.

Beyond and above the hall, towering in the distance, the mountain peaks shone brilliant in the midday sun . . .

The cottage was on the south side of the camp. It was only a few minutes' walk away and, had it not been for the boundary wall, we would certainly have seen it before.

The family who lived there welcomed us like long-lost brothers, hugged us, sat us down in the best chairs, served us immediately with hot bean soup and subjected us to a torrent of chatter. Doubtless Maria had told them I spoke Italian, but it was one thing to utter a few halting words and quite another to interpret this fast flow of Ascoli-Piceno dialect.

Their tone of voice, at least, betokened their friendliness.

The nonno was more than slightly deaf, so the three children took turns in telling him our story over and over again. By the time we'd downed our minestra the seventeen days had grown to around three weeks under the weighbridge!

Their father presently quietened them with a reproving gesture and pointed to the clock.

"Un' ora!" he announced and switched on the battery wireless. Whereupon, still as statues, they gazed apprehensively at the crackling receiver.

Hal and I well understood the anxiety of these people waiting for the war to surge through their village and engulf their farms and their homes. The possibilities were terrible to contemplate: destruction by the retreating Germans or by the advancing British or in the bloody turmoil of battle. How fervently must they be praying for the fighting to pass them by!

Where were the Allies? We had lived every day expecting their arrival, listening for the thunder of guns and roar of aircraft. The tranquillity suggested that our troops were farther away than we had been led to believe.

The annunciatore spoke of the Penisola di Gargarno, of Foggia and of the battle for Termoli. He also referred to the River Biferno and I distinguished the word "torrente".

The ultimate switching-off by Papa was the signal for the two youngest children to begin playing a repulsive war-game, machine-gunning indiscriminately.

CHAPTER 19   THE CONTADINI

At that moment the door-latch clicked. Conversation ceased. Everyone looked at everyone else in alarm, and at the opening door.

A dapper, bright-eyed man entered carrying a basket of apples.

He exchanged greetings with the family, gave the children an apple apiece, and addressed me.

"Mi chiamo Primo — Marcelli Primo."

I introduced Hal as Aroldo, and myself as Arturo. I knew of no Italian form of "Kenneth" so decided to use my first Christian name "Arthur".

While the family were repeating our names I asked Primo:

"Quanto chilometri Termoli?"

"Two 'undred!" he replied, dolefully shaking his head, "English take long time. Il fiume è in torrente, capito? Impossibile traversare!"

It was a crushing disappointment. Atkinson's announcement had led us to believe that our army was in the vicinity, advancing with all speed. Now we were faced with the brutal truth. They were bogged down the other side of the River Biferno one-hundred-and-fifty miles away!

We realised that the rivers were swollen, both with rain and with the melting snow of the Appenines.

There followed an animated dialogue between Papa and Primo during which the latter three times repeated:

*"Tedeschi in vicino — pericoloso stare qui."

Finally Papa shrugged his shoulders and nodded. Then he came across to us and shook our hands.

"A rivederci Inglesi e buona fortuna!" It was a reluctant goodbye.

Primo beckoned us as the women once again loaded our possessions onto their heads.

We made our way up the hillside, ahead of us the distant Appenine peaks which for me had always symbolised freedom. About half-way up we came to a tiny stone cottage — to be exact, a pair of semi-detached two-room cottages.

We approached through the garden where a vine, arching over, formed a complete umbrella of grapes. At the edge of this a number of pigs were rooting around in a sizeable stye.

Watching us from the doorway of one of the cottages was a tall well-built man of around sixty years of age.

"Ciao Alfredo!" greeted Primo, "Ecco i due prigioneri inglesi."

Having escaped from the prison camp, albeit with some help from the contadine, I was slightly piqued at being referred to as a prisoner.

Alfredo lumbered towards us, and it was only then I noticed that his trousers were tied in beneath the knee of his left leg. Below that was only a shiny black wooden stump.

†"L'ho perduto nella guerra di quattordici — diciotto," he told us.

* Germans in the district — dangerous to stay here.
† I lost it in the 14-18 war.

123

Primo nodded sympathetically as he put down the basket of apples near the cottage entrance.

"For you," he said, smiling at Hal and me. Our heartfelt "Mille grazie!" was not only for Primo but also for the women now carrying our belongings into the cottage adjoining Alfredo's.

The two men remained talking a few minutes while inside the cottage the women were conversing excitedly.

Presently came the leave-taking.

"Arrivederci Aroldo: Arrivederci Arturo!" called out Maria.

"Arrivederci Inglesi!" echoed the laughing women returning down into the valley.

"Ciao!" grinned Primo. Then, agile as a mountain-goat, he was climbing the slope towards the tomato-patch. We watched him until he had disappeared among the trees near the crest of the hill.

Alfredo grinned and placed his arm on Hal's shoulder.

"Now I show you where to go if tedeschi come."

He led us to the stye. We stepped over and round the occupants, stooping to enter the covered section.

With his stump he pointed to the muddy straw.

*"Guarda sotto la paglia!"

Hal bent down and moved the straw aside. Even then the muddied trap-door was difficult to distinguish from the surrounding earth floor.

Finding the edge, Hal lifted out the oblong panel. Below it was a pit big enough to conceal two or three people.

Alfredo's stump rapped a lug on the underside of the trap.

"Of course," said Hal, "That'll be for closing or opening it from underneath."

"If tedeschi come, you hide — capito?" The old man chuckled, repeated the word "tedeschi", spat and then led the way back to the cottage.

He held open the door for us. The ground floor room was empty — stone floor, stone walls, large open stone fireplace where hung a cauldron, and not a stick of furniture. The place had evidently not been lived in for some time. We climbed the narrow stone steps to the bedroom where we were gratified to see a bed. The women had made it up with our palliasses and blankets from the camp. Against the wall they had bestowed our other belongings.

When we went downstairs Alfredo had gone.

The room was empty except for the basket of apples now perched on the wide stone window-sill. We chose one each and strolled out into the grape-festooned garden.

Below us the curved roofs of the prison-compounds glinted in the afternoon sun; the slender water-tower shone like a stylized rose; at this distance even the puny trees in the garden glowed with a delicate gold-green loveliness.

* Look under the straw.

CHAPTER 19   THE CONTADINI

As for the barbed wire, it was now scarcely visible — no more than an exquisite border-pattern in finest etching.

We threw our cores to the pigs and, above their noisy grunting, failed to hear the approaching footsteps.

"Aroldo! Arturo! 'Allo!" The voice startled us, sounding so close in our ears. We were relieved that it was none other than Maria accompanied by her friends. That they had departed towards the valley and returned from the upper slopes was explained by the fact that now they carried piles of brushwood. All except Maria who balanced an ewer of water on her head. They had made a detour in the woods to gather kindling.

Into our cottage they went, arranging their burdens on the hearth. In no time at all Maria had emptied the ewer into the cauldron and her friends had got a roaring fire going.

Then one of the women flashed a saucy look at me, murmuring something to her companions which sent them into fits of laughter. To me she uttered only one word, "Camicia."

While I was wondering just what it meant, she stepped forward boldly and, amid shrieks of merriment from the others, began unbuttoning my khaki shirt.

"Bisogna tingerla, Arturo," explained Maria, accepting Hal's shirt which he'd already stripped off.

"They're going to dye them for us, Ken."

I followed Hal's example, removing the only item of clothing I was wearing that identified me as British. Our pale green trousers were Italian issue. As for footwear, as both Primo and Alfredo wore British-Army style boots, we imagined that many other Italians did likewise. Maybe they had been bought on the Black Market or maybe filched from a parcel. So many Red Cross bulk consignments had been pilfered, so few "personal" parcels had ever arrived at the camp. However, it could have been that Italian-Army boots were of similar pattern.

When the cauldron began steaming, the women poured in dyes from two little bottles and stirred the concoction awhile. Then they threw in our shirts, pushing them down into the simmering liquid with the stirrer — a long stick they had brought with them.

We tried to thank them but they laughingly ushered us out into the garden. Maria saying:

"Via! Via! Andate prendere un bagno di sole. Non c'è posto qui."

Indeed there was not room for the six of us in the tiny kitchen. It was a joy to walk out under the vine, plucking handfuls of grapes before seeking a patch of lush grass whereon to sunbathe.

So we lazed away our first afternoon of freedom that October day enjoying the golden season which in Ascoli divides summer from autumn.

I was only half-awake and Hal peacefully sleeping when the contadine brought out our now dark brown shirts, spreading them on the nearby bushes to dry.

ESCAPE FROM ASCOLI

A friendly wave of the stirrer-stick from Maria, who was also carrying the empty ewer on her head, and then the four of them, sure-footed and elegant in their stride, were departing.

I watched them down into the valley, listening until their ceaseless chatter faded. When they turned along the road leading to the camp, they disappeared abruptly in the dip. Only the ewer was visible, gliding smoothly along the bank towards the cluster of buildings that had recently confined 8000 British prisoners-of-war . . .

Near-at-hand the last tenuous wisps of wood-smoke lingered above the cottage chimney before vanishing completely . . .

We went early to bed that evening for, in spite of our siesta, we were both exceedingly tired.

CHAPTER 20

Walk before breakfast

The next morning and each morning thereafter bevies of teenage girls arrived bringing us food sent by their families. They carried it, not on their heads but in baskets hooked over their arms. On Thursday there were four girls, round-eyed and serious; on Friday they brought two gigglers for company; on Saturday there were seven; while on Sunday the little cottage was a cornucopia of young females and food — bread, eggs and fruit mostly, with bottles of vino crudo.

We learnt that, by order of the authorities, all schools had long since been closed. Educational establishments were centres of opposition to the Fascist regime.

We were deeply moved by the kindness of these people. At the same time we were concerned that so much activity at a supposedly-empty cottage might arouse the suspicions of our enemies.

"I'm sure the novelty will wear off," declared Hal.

But he proved wrong. The girls came each day of the next week openly carrying our provender.

On the night of Friday, 22nd October we were awakened by the growl of heavy trucks on the road. From the little bedroom window we saw the front of the camp illuminated by the approaching headlights of three vehicles. Then the engines were switched off and snatches of German conversation drifted up to us.

However the presence of the tedeschi made not the slightest difference. The ragazze visited us just the same, only in greater numbers.

Something had to be done in the interests of security. To our delight Primo turned up on the Monday. We explained our predicament: so many people thronging the "empty" cottage with the Germans only some three hundred yards away down in the valley.

He, too, was alarmed by the situation and promised to arrange to move us elsewhere as soon as possible. He also said he would ask the local families to make their visits less obtrusive.

We were sure he found this a difficult task. The generosity of these warm-hearted folk was so abundant and every family for miles around was anxious to contribute towards our well-being.

However for each of the remaining week-days of October we received no more than two ragazze who stayed only briefly. On the other hand Primo

127

was quite unable to get the youngsters to stay away on Sundays, and on the 24th and 31st we were more crowded than ever.

Fortunately the tedeschi were seldom about during daytime — just bringing in their trucks at night and driving away early in the morning.

After they had gone Hal and I would walk up to the top of the hill. From there we could look upon the brightly-coloured patchwork of fields spread across the steep slopes on the opposite side of the camp, or turn to gaze at the rugged peaks to the west.

Often we heard far-off explosions.

"Do you think our troops are somewhere in the area?" I asked.

Hal shook his head.

"No hope of that. You know very well from the radio that they're near Termoli at least 150 miles away."

"But it sounds like the rumble of gunfire. Perhaps it's a group of Italian partisans at firing practice?"

"Perhaps!" said Hal drily . . .

On 27th and 28th we didn't leave the shelter of the cottage because Alfredo said a band of Fascisti had just arrived from Ancona looking for Italian Army deserters.

"I tell you when to 'ide!" he said, jerking his thumb towards the pigstye.

In fact the Fascists didn't come to Monte Urano. Rumour had it that at nearby Sant' Elpidio they had arrested a man who had almost immediately escaped. They'd departed northwards in pursuit.

Those two October days were gloriously sunny and we sat in Alfredo's little vineyard listening to his stories about his experiences in the First World War — how he'd survived the murderous battles unscathed only to have the misfortune to be drinking at an inn when it was demolished by a stray shell.

He also told us about the days when the prison camp was a linificio and how they separated the seed from the fibre. We gathered that both seed and fibre were transported by rail to the linseed-oil and linen factory. Listening to Alfredo was no passive occupation. From the time when he fought — or drank — side by side with the Tommies he had culled a few words of English so that communication was an hilarious pantomime of gesticulation accompanied by a mystifying hotch-potch of strangely-pronounced English and dialect Italian. For example:

"Two buoi" (Two fingers raised and head down like an ox pulling a wagon), "trarravano the carrot," (meaning "cart"), "a-stoppa-pesare il lino," (stop to weigh the flax) "ow many chilogrammi, per esempio," (mime of a needle moving round a dial).

Communication was a slow but very friendly process whereby it took a whole morning to convey that which would normally be said in half-an-hour. It also required frequent vino-lubrication so that by midday a pleasant conviviality was achieved.

On Monday, All-Saints' Day, rain streaming down his chirpy face, our own particular saint arrived — our trusty friend Marcelli Primo.

CHAPTER 20   WALK BEFORE BREAKFAST

"Tomorrow morning very early I take you to a very nice family. Be ready for five o'clock."

We thanked him and asked if there were any further news of the English advance. His reply, as water dripped from his long black impermeabile, was to walk two fingers slowly along our stone window-sill and mutter, "Piano-piano! piano-piano! Ancora in vicino Termoli."

It was that sort of advance — little by very little.

He went next-door to chat with Alfredo before returning over the hill . . .

It was exactly five o'clock by Hal's watch when, the following morning from the bedroom window, we saw him descending the hill, easily recognisable by his jaunty stride.

We donned our thick Army pullovers, still khaki because the contadine had thought that in that mild season, we weren't likely to have immediate need of them. Then we picked up our belongings, all except the palliasses and blankets, and opened the cottage-door just as Primo was about to knock. We noticed that he was carrying a large torch.

"Come quickly!" he whispered, "There are many tedeschi in the valley!"

We followed him up the slope; hastening through the shadows of early morning which lurked in spinneys and woods; scrambling up and down steep wet banks; slithering on muddy paths articulate with running water; sometimes leaping across or wading through wider streams.

It was an hour and a half before Primo finally stopped, allowing us a minute's rest.

"Very good this lampadina," he said, switching it on. Even in the dawn-light it was dazzling. "If we meet Fascisti I shine it in face — so!" He beamed it into my eyes and I could see nothing. "When I say 'Buon' giorno!' they know my voice. They think, 'Is only old Primo the fruitseller. Is harmless!' and they not see you properly."

"But suppose the trick doesn't work?" objected Hal, the pessimist.

Primo chuckled:

"Is heavy — la lampadina!" and using it like a cosh, he struck a couple of twigs off a nearby birch-tree.

We were on the lip of a wide valley into which we descended to follow a country road. The crunch of our footsteps was accompanied by the trickle of water flowing in deep ditches on either side. We came to a grumbling water-mill, then crossed a river by a white-railed bridge. Presently, after turning right at a junction, we met an old man carrying a sack. Primo shone his torch to blind him to our khaki pullovers and greeted him with a friendly "Ciao Tomasso"

A few minutes later he gripped my arm and led me abruptly off the road down a muddy farm-track. We squelched past a small vegetable garden and through an apple-orchard onto a cobbled yard. Here stamping the muck from our boots, we aroused a skelter of hens who announced our arrival with such a cackling as must surely have alerted the whole neighbourhood.

In front of us was a long building of mellow stone. At the end nearest us there were three small upstairs windows, one of which had been bricked in. At farmyard level we saw two large wooden double-door entrances which may have been stables, and one single-door entrance which we guessed led to a store-room.

Two stone steps led up to a pair of smaller doors. These were pushed open to reveal a man of medium height clad in dark corduroys and bright blue shirt. His face was wreathed in a welcoming smile. Even in that early morning light the blue of his eyes seemed brighter even than the blue of his shirt.

Primo introduced us, saying:

"Aroldo — Arturo — Pacifico Brugnoni."

After shaking hands our new acquaintance corrected, pointing to himself:

"Non sono Pacifico. Mi chiamo Pace." He pronounced his name "Pah-chay"

Behind Pace were more stone steps, a flight of them leading up to a wire-meshed gate. Beyond this was a plain wooden door already open just wide enough for a small face to be peeping round the edge of it.

We went upsteps following Pace, pigeons flapping round our heads, poultry scuttling between our feet. Once at the top Pace deftly opened the gate, shooing away the birds.

"Porca matosca!" swore Primo, also angrily waving his arms as the beating wings brushed by him.

The small face swung inwards as we entered.

Its owner, a little girl of about seven, scampered across the stone-paved kitchen floor into the arms of a jolly-looking woman who was holding a clove of garlic in her hand.

Then a man stepped forward to greet us. He closely resembled Pace and was obviously his younger brother.

"Io Gino, fratello di Pace," he said, warmly shaking hands.

Gino's shirt was the same blue as Pace's — perhaps the same dye; his eyes, although dark in colour, shone with the same remarkable brightness; he also was clean-shaven, but there was a pucker of laughter in his features which counter-balanced Pace's more serious demeanour.

Pace then took my arm to complete the introductions.

"Ines, mia moglie," His wife, a brown-eyed slender woman, threw another bundle of sticks on the fire before standing up, smoothing her apron and nodding to us. There was a hint of sadness in her smile.

"Moglie di Gino, Stella." Gino's wife, cheerful and voluptuous, chuckled in rich dialect.

"Primo tell me about you. Cattivi! What you do with all those ragazze at the cottage?" Then releasing the little girl and addressing her "Di Buon giorno, Caterina!"

Caterina needed no further bidding. She ran to us joyfully.

"Buon-giorno-Aroldo-buon-giorno-Arturo!"

As she spoke her little hand clutched mine. She led me across to a wrinkled old lady who was sieving corn. On her head she wore a kind of black hood. Her spindly legs were clad in coarse black stockings, black sandals on her feet.

"Prozia Assunta!" she chirrupped.

Assunta looked at us briefly, pityingly, her wrinkles quivering; then quickly bent over her work. She was weeping and her words were scarcely audible.

*"Poveri! poveri! — E poveri noi!"

Caterina kissed her great-aunt and took me across to the hearth where, amply-swaddled and wedged in a curious upright wooden box, was a gurgling baby.

"Mia piccola sorella," said Caterina proudly, "Romana."

* Poor devils — And poor us!

CHAPTER 21

The priest and the nun

The water in the pot was bubbling.

Old Assunta put down the sieve, picked up a jug and hurried across to dip out some boiling water, returned to her workbench and set about making acorn coffee.

Pace rubbed his hands in anticipation and took his place in the chair at the head of a long table. It was solidly made, that table, of oak and occupying half the length of the kitchen; its surface, beautifully smooth and scrupulously clean.

Ines sat down on the bench on Pace's right, Gino and Stella in the chairs on his left. Primo, accepting the Brugnoni's invitation, ensconced himself beside Ines.

"Vieni Arturo! Aroldo vieni!" called out Stella flapping her hand at us while Ines got up again in order to help Assunta.

No sooner had we seated ourselves next to Primo than Assunta placed mugs of steaming caffe latte in front of us, answering our thanks with:

"Prego, Aroldo! Prego, Arturo!"

It was a poor substitute coffee but the friendliness with which it was given made it one of the choicest brews ever. And the latte, udder-fresh, improved it enormously.

Despite the fact that it was not yet 7 a.m. the conversation was lively and full of fun although scarcely intelligible to me. As yet my ear was not properly attuned to the Ascoli-Piceno dialect but I sensed that we had immediately been accepted as members of the family, and marvelled at their gaiety in the face of the dangers they were running.

I leaned back against the stone wall and examined the kitchen. Above me, evenly spaced along the length of the ceiling, were five sturdy wooden arches with their transverses, with five horizontal beams on either side. Somebody must once have made the mistake of painting these timbers for flakes of white still clung to them.

Facing me was an enormous brick-and-stone fireplace above which at the middle of a high mantelpiece stood an ancient coffee-grinder. From the crackling wood-fire blue veins of smoke reached up to mingle with steam rising from a simmering cauldron. This was suspended by hook and chain and, hanging on wooden pegs in the brickwork were chains of various thicknesses, hooks of various sizes, a toothed spit, a ladle and a large frying-pan.

133

To the left was an oblong construction of stone and brick. It was about three-foot high, its top about eighteen inches square. Therein was a recess into which, as we later discovered, hot embers were shovelled and on which a metal grill was placed. Leaning against the chimney-breast nearby was a wafter — that is to say, a stick with a bundle of large feathers tied to the end.

The whole of the right-hand end of the hearth was taken up with a pile of brushwood.

Shelves were built-in to the left of the fireplace, and, down towards the end of the kitchen near the sink, a row for cutlery and scoops. Lined up on the floor nearby were three ewers and in front of a small window, a dresser or "madia" where the flour was stored. On top was a box of salt, jars of tomato puree and one jar of peach jam.

The window, like all the other windows, was protected by wire-netting and shutters. Even so, pigeons managed to force an entry from time to time.

In the days to come Pace or Gino repaired the wire several times. But the pigeons, being strong, determined birds, soon hammered out another opening. Flapping pigeons were the accepted accompaniment of a meal at the Brugnoni's. My personal pigeon would from time to time alight on my shoulder and coo affectionately into my ear.

That morning of Tuesday, 2nd November Hal and I seemed suddenly to have stepped right back into the Middle Ages. Just as we marvelled at the overwhelming kindness of the contadini, so also were we amazed at the utter simplicity of their way of life: no electricity, no gas, no piped water, no carpets, no easy chairs nor settees — none of the comforts English families of the period took for granted.

The door opened and a laughing, tousle-haired youth appeared amid a flurry of poultry. He called out something to Pace who got up abruptly, saying:

"Subito, subito, Agostino!"

Thereupon the whole family finished off their coffee and set to work: Assunta clearing the table, Ines making for the outer door followed by the men.

Stella crossed to the fireplace, picked up an empty ewer and beckoned to us. We followed her down the flight of steps, out into the cobbled yard, turning right to go to the front of the farm-house where there was a well. She placed the ewer in position and filled it from the bucket, splashing her bare feet in the process.

When the ewer was full I stepped forward, offering to carry it for her but she grinned and shook her head. From somewhere she produced a small kerchief, twisted it into a ring and placed it on her head exactly as Maria and her friends had done at the prison-camp. On this she perched the ewer and set off back towards the house.

On the way she passed Agostino who was carrying two heavy buckets. They spoke to each other and laughed but we heard neither words nor laughter because just then the oxen set up a chorus of bellowing. They must have scented either Agostino or the contents of his buckets.

He pushed open a door and stood there waiting for us.

My first impression on entering the stall was that I'd happened upon a church crypt. The low vaulted stone arches and pillars were just the same, as indeed was the semi-obscurity. But the two tiny windows were rectangular, not arched; the air not dank and sepulchral but warm and pungent with the breath and bodies of animals; the whole place with its paraphernalia of boxes, rope, tools and bench and generously-laid straw had a homeliness emphasised by half a dozen pairs of tranquil bovine eyes. The ground floor of this podere was home for the animals just as upstairs was home for human beings. Both had their rights.

Agostino, who as far as we knew was not related to the family, introduced us to each of the buoi in turn as he emptied out their portions of fodder from the buckets. Fine docile beasts they were, one pure white and the others white with tawny patches.

When the buckets were emptied, the two of us took them out to the well where Hal and I rinsed them.

Presently Agostino joined us.

He pointed to the house.

"That is where you sleep," he informed us, indicating the third in the row of seven windows. The first window gave light to the staircase, the second to the kitchen. This was therefore the first of the bedrooms.

We sauntered round to the yard where Ines was throwing handfuls of corn to the poultry. Like Stella, indeed like all the contadine women except Assunta, she went barefoot at her work.

Presently as the noisy squawking subsided we heard a whistle from the direction of the orchard. A man's voice called out "Grego! Grego, vieni qui!" and from the fields to our right there appeared a long, lean brown dog. He bounded up to Pace, for it was he, and followed him across the yard and into the house.

"Come now to have fagioli," Ines invited.

We returned up the stone stairway to the kitchen where the family were once again assembling at that beautiful long oak table.

"Fagioli" turned out to be a piping hot bean soup which we took with bread and the inevitable vino crudo.

Grego introduced himself, sniffing each of us briefly before attending to a dish of raw meat awaiting him beside the fireplace. We wondered why we hadn't heard him when we had first arrived.

Pace explained that he was an outdoor dog and that he would have been guarding the sheep.

"If anyone go near the sheep then Grego very fierce!" added Gino, showing his teeth and rolling his eyes.

His colazione finished, Grego stretched his uttermost length on the hearth, lay down his head and closed his eyes. He took no notice when Assunta took Hal's plate to the hanging pot to scoop out a second helping of fagioli.

"Permesso!" chirped little Caterina to her mother, got down from the table and ran across to squat beside Grego and stroke his head. The dog's only response was to flick his left ear.

At the same time the swaddled Romana, upright in her "baby-box" began uttering little cries to the effect that, if this were feeding-time, she preferred not to be left out. Accordingly Stella came across, lifted her up into her arms and, cooing and crooning, carried her through to the bedrooms.

Ines watched them go, then said abruptly:

"Arturo, Aroldo! — Come, I show you your bedroom."

There was a catch in her voice that was nearly a sob and Pace glanced at her tenderly. In that moment I understood that her sadness was the sadness of a childless wife.

Agostino's information proved correct: ours was the first room on our left, furnished with an enormous brass bed, a wooden chest and a home-made wash-stand complete with jug, bowl and vaso da notte. Ines frowned at our khaki pullovers.

"Maybe we dye those," she said, then with a smiling "A rivederci subito," she left us to bestow our paltry belongings.

For a few minutes I sat on the wide stone sill looking out on the farm. A rough track, lined with lime-trees threaded nearby fields of fennel and corn, ran down yellow and straight past the sheep-meadows and lost itself in a long fringe of woodland. Further along the valley I glimpsed the river*, doubtless the one we'd crossed by the white-railed bridge. It glinted like polished steel in the early sun.

An old man in a floppy straw hat was placing a short ladder against the nearest of the lime-trees as Caterina went racing towards him.

Then Ines and Stella appeared carrying baskets and Caterina was looking up at me beckoning.

When we went out to join them, it was once again Caterina who made the introductions:

"Nonno Francesco." Grandfather Brugnoni shook hands, his left hand still resting on the ladder. Like Pace and Gino, his eyes were bright and penetrating.

"Cugina Vincensina."

Vincensina emerged from her hiding-place in the finocchio-field, carefully repeated our names and shook hands.

"A-roldo, buon' giorno. Ar-turo, buon' giorno."

Then while Francesco steadied the ladder, the two women climbed up into the tree and began plucking the tender leaves.

"Per i buoi." explained Caterina, halfway up the ladder bending down a

* River Tenna

136

low branch on which Francesco hung an empty sack. Then the old man grinned at us and translated proudly, "Feed oxens!"

The contadine worked deftly and quickly. When their baskets were full they emptied them into the sack. When the sack was full, Francesco bore it away and hung an empty one in its place. Harvesting the limetree-leaves was a task which, on and off, occupied the whole of that week.

The next day, Wednesday, was the day of the breadmaking. The flour, Pace told us, was from their own corn, their farm yielding twelve quintals per annum.

We found old Francesco, still straw-hatted, in the family's bakehouse adjoining the horse's stable. He was feeding sticks and dried maize stalks into the brick oven. There was no thermometer but when he judged the temperature right, he raked the embers to one side, calling:

"Olà! Pronto, pronto!"

At this Ines and Stella came in carrying a long board on which were pizze ready for baking. This they carefully set down on nearby trestles.

With his baker's paddle Francesco slid in each pizza in turn to rest on the clay floor beside the embers. Then he clanged shut the oven door. The women departed with the empty board to fetch the dough, a simple mix of flour and water. When a few minutes later they returned with a boardful of cloth-wrapped loaves for baking, Francesco was already taking the pizze from the oven and dropping them into a shallow round basket.

*"Adesso la temperatura è giusta per il pane," he explained, paddling the loaves in, the sweat bedewing his wrinkles.

"Bread ready one hour." . . .

We spent that hour with Agostino, cutting straw for the oxen from a stack near the other end of the house. Afterwards with three-tined prongs we loaded it into baskets. Carrying these round to the oxen we savoured the aroma of the freshly-baked bread, held our breath in the pungent stall, then hurried back to watch Francesco laying out the loaves on the board. Never was bread so evenly-baked — no black or pale patches to spoil the appetising golden-brown crust.

At two o'clock we ate a hunk of it with our minestra and declared it the most delicious we had ever tasted . . .

In the afternoon we helped clean out a shallow fossa beside the trees despite the protests of seventeen-year old Agostino who had just descried his girl-friend, Carla, working in a field on the other side of the river.

"Per irrigazione," said Gino, winking and turning his back on the lovesick boy whose dark mop of hair flopped to the rhythm of his hoe.

Although nine years his elder I felt sympathy for Agostino and, later that day, showed him the biscuit-tin-framed photo of my love . . .

Work finished as daylight began to fade and after seven o'clock supper, the oil-lamps lit, we all gathered round the great chimney-piece to chat.

* Now the temperature's right for the bread.

137

ESCAPE FROM ASCOLI

Stella teased us about the matrimoniale, meaning the bed, capacious enough for couples to disport themselves in every possible position. Then from a corner of the kitchen she produced an elliptical frame of wooden laths. Chuckling, she placed this on the hearth, lifting off the top section. Fitted to a pillar at the middle of the lower part was a wooden tray about 25 centimetres square.

"Ecco la monica. Arturo!" chuckled Stella.

My bewilderment must have shown for the frame could have been mistaken for the fuselage of a model aeroplane but in no way at all did it put me in mind of a holy nun.

Meanwhile Stella stooped before the fire to shovel red-hot embers into a shallow earthenware pot which I hadn't noticed before. The pot had a handle and resembled a small frying-pan.

"Anche ecco il prete, Arturo."

The pot of embers was the priest.

Rolling her eyes wickedly, Stella laid il prete on the platform inside la monica and replaced the top of the frame.

"To warm your bed!" shrieked Francesco, tears shining in his bright eyes. With a wistful smile Ines picked up the prete-e-monica and carried it through to our bedroom.

After which ribaldry, Pace led the family prayers.

And so to bed, the most efficiently-warmed bed we'd ever known for the monica held the bedclothes open to allow the priest's passionate warmth to reach its farthest corners.

CHAPTER 22

Contadino with bike

During those November days I did my utmost to become a contadino myself, volunteering for all the tasks of the farm — mucking out stall and stable, fetching tubs of grain and feeding it into the oblong sowing-box, hitching the oxen to the sower-shaft by hole and wooden peg and learning to lead the oxen.

My first job with the oxen was to gather up some yellow weed from a meadow and load it into a cart. Very good fodder, Pace had said.

"Oo-laa!" I yelled. The chocolate-brown ox, Battista, trudged forward to the first pile of cut weed. "Lei-ii!" I commanded. She halted and waited while I tossed the weed in with my prong.

Then she turned her head towards the rain-washed hedge which, like all the hedges in the district, was largely composed of vine. She sniffed. She bellowed appreciatively and, without more ado, lumbered across and began to chew the succulent leaves and small green grapes.

"Le-ii!" I screamed. She took no notice, tucking in voraciously.

"Oo-laa!" I ventured. At that she moved, but only farther along the hedge where she shoved her head forward and got herself entangled in the twisting branches.

"Come back, you stupid brute!" I pleaded all-too-politely.

Hearing the English, she paused, defecated copiously, then nuzzled the delicious leaves with renewed eagerness, more snagged-up than ever.

Just then, to my immense relief, Pace came striding through the woodland on the far side of the hedge. He glared at Battista through a gap in the vine.

"Porco-Dio!"

I'd never heard anybody swear with such ferocity. The effect on the ox was incredible. She stopped chewing, gazed apologetically at Pace, extricated herself, backed away, turned and obediently pulled the cart forward to the next weed-pile. There she waited for me to continue the day's labours. That was another laugh at supper-time. Despite this disaster Pace gave me charge of the oxen for an hour's seed-sowing and on another day for grass-cutting. On these occasions they behaved impeccably, perhaps because first time the dog, Grego, was present as bird-scarer, and second time Gino, Agostino and Hal as grassrakers.

I did as Gino had instructed me, starting at the centre of the field and working outwards. At the end of each strip I raised the cutter, put the

139

machine "in dietro", turned, pushed the cutter-lever forward and set off once more.

And once more I proved my inefficiency as farm-labourer — this time by failing to slow down the oxen where the grass grew thickest. The resistance was too much for the cutters which thereupon ate into the ground and got thoroughly clogged.

At such times Hal's mechanical expertise was invaluable. He dismantled the machine, freed the saw-toothed horizontal cutters, knocked out the dents caused by the stones and re-assembled it all within the space of half-an-hour!

After securing the shaft with peg and ring. Gino shouted "Oo-laa!" and the oxen plodded forward immediately. His face was a picture as he watched the now-quiet-moving machine lay flat the whispering swathes.

On 5th November Gino hitched an ox to a V-shaped wooden plough exactly like those used in Ancient Greece. He then ploughed a small field bordering the river. The next day we sowed fave (beans) for fodder for the old black horse.

Two black-clad fishermen in waders stood in the river idly watching.

*"Non si preoccupi!" muttered Gino, but I was glad that un-Italian-looking Hal wasn't with us at the time. Then it was Gino's turn to swear at the top of his voice to the ox: "Porco-Dio!" The beast was eating the beans we'd just sowed!

This juxtaposition of pig and God was for the Italians the most shocking expletive. They were amused at the English fashion of swearing by the sexual act. It seemed so inappropriate after, for example, hitting one's thumb with a hammer!

When working near the trees Gino was always on the look-out for pieces of wood suitable for whittling with his beautiful penknife. Dextrously he sculpted soldiers, dolls and animals. It took him all his spare moments but the finished articles were exquisite. Whenever any of the children happened along he was quick to hide his current work of art.

He it was who cut the family's hair. With no other tools but scissors and comb, he achieved results equal to Jim Mackay's in the POW camp. In any event, both Jim and Gino would put to shame many a top stylist. I've never had the job done better . . .

While we were gathering brushwood for the fire one day, we were alarmed by a sudden burst of firing close at hand. I was about to drop flat on the ground but Gino only grinned, repeating:

"Non si preoccupi! E la caccia al fagiano"

Shooting pheasants not peasants, thank God!

However we did notice Gino sometimes wince at frequent distant heavy gunfire.

* Don't worry!

*"La Regia Marina Inglese!" he once explained, a certain note of bitterness in his voice . . .

On Thursday evenings we helped Pace load the brightly-painted cart with bundles of finocchio. Finocchio (fennel) was one of the principal saleable crops and fetched one lira a bundle, a lira being worth twopence-halfpenny in English money of the period. It grew about 3-foot tall. With bread and vino crudo it turned up almost inevitably as our lunchtime diet. Apart from the morning colazione of bean soup, cooking was usually for the evening.

One sunny morning the women took our thick pullovers for dying.

"Andate fare un passeggiata," Ines suggested, almost echoing the words of Maria at the hillside cottage. Whereupon she plunged the khaki woollies into the bubbling pot.

We did as we were told, strolling down to the long meadow near the river.

"Long enough for a D.H. Rapide to land and take off," I observed wistfully.

"Don't let's kid ourselves!" retorted Hal, "We've no chance of an air rescue." . . .

Ines and Stella were coming down the stairway when we got back to the house. Poultry scattered in all directions as they crossed the yard, taking the steaming baskets over to the clothes-line near the orchard.

The clothes they pegged out were now a delicious chocolate colour: the tell-tale khaki was gone.

We still wore the same Italian-issue cotton trousers.

Likewise every Monday Stella would ask:

"Arturo! Aroldo! Fazzoletti? Anche altre cose? È giorno di bucato." Washing day!

Then she and Ines, accompanied by Caterina, would make their way down the lime-tree path to the river, carrying on their heads the baskets of washing, a bar of soap in each. On the way they were always joined by Caterina's nine-year-old cousin, Vincensina, who had come across the fields to take part in the "bucato" with her mother, Giovanna and her grown-up sisters, Movidia and Giuseppina.

While the children helped or played, the chattering women would be kneeling on the bank or standing in the river. They rinsed the linen in the water fast-flowing from the Appenines, they beat it with large pebbles, they thoroughly soaped it, rinsed it again — exactly as their forebears had done for centuries. The resulting cleanliness was a joy to behold! . . .

The best way I could repay the kindness of the contadini was to teach their children for it was a great sadness at that time that all schools had been ordered to close. The class varied. If the Germans or fascisti were in the district there was no class at all. When conditions were favourable the roll comprised Caterina, Vincensina, Marcelli Primo's 10-year old son Pierrino, and two or three children from the Tre-Tre and Marinello families.

* The Royal Navy

141

ESCAPE FROM ASCOLI

The schoolroom was the Brugnoni's kitchen, the little pupils gathered round that beautiful long table. Lessons proceeded with old Assunta clattering and wheezing between the sink and the fireplace as she prepared the meals.

As from time to time she gave the children "bocconcin!" (tasters), the cooking aroma helped rather than hindered our studies. Except on one memorable afternoon!

Pierrino broke off from reading about Garibaldi to exclaim, "Poh!"

"Oibo!" echoed Vincensina, looking across disgustedly at the huge black pot.

"Auf!" from Caterina, screwing up her face. The other children were holding their noses.

"Che puzzo!" added Pierrino, fanning himself with his dog-eared Fascist-inspired history reader.

Assunta cackled and beckoned me to help her. She made me add various items to the unsavoury mixture — a table-spoonful of salt, some olive oil, a pinch of herbs and tiny quantities of ingredients I couldn't identify.

Then she asked me to give it a good stir.

While I was thus occupied she went over to speak to the children, doubtless to re-assure them.

But, instead of calming down, the children began shrieking with laughter and, when I turned round, I saw that Assunta was laughing too.

"We no eat that, Arturo," said Pierrino in his best English "Eet ees soap!"

Later that day Assunta turned it out into a large shallow dish and when, with cooling, it had sufficiently hardened, she cut it into slabs — long green bars like the ones we saw poking out of the washing baskets on the day of the bucato . . .

The following Thursday evening, the cart having been loaded with finocchio, Pace beckoned me into the stable. I thought he wished me to renew my acquaintance with the old black horse, but Pace only patted him absent-mindedly. Then he looked me straight in the eyes and asked:

"You ride bicycle?"

I knew in that moment that, although Pace would have liked us to stay for ever, he more than any of the family understood our need to escape from Occupied Italy. When I nodded in reply he led me to the back of the stable where, suspended by hooks and ropes was a bicycle the like of which I'd never set eyes on outside a museum — a sit-up-and-beg, the frame colourful as an ice-cream cart and as elegantly fashioned.

As I helped him lift it down, he said:

"Francesco no ride it anymore."

I tried to thank him but he just clapped me on the shoulder, murmured, "Domani you ride it, Arturo," ushered me out of the stable and bolted the doors . . .

"Now you can reconnoitre the area, find out if there really are many Germans about," said Hal next morning.

An eight-kilometre ride along the country road took me to the autostrada which runs down the Adriatic coast. It was teeming with tedeschi, but overcoming my terror, I turned south along it, passing the railway station at Porto San Giorgio.

A seemingly-endless slow-moving column of Panzers and trucks was thundering down towards the line.

Somehow I got wedged between a tank behind and a truck in front. I was cursing my foolhardiness when a German sergeant in the truck waved to me, grinned and threw me three of packets of cigarettes!

Waving back my thanks I wobbled to the edge of the highway, dismounted and plucked them out of the path of the approaching tank caterpillars.

When I eventually got back, Pace and Hal were hugely delighted with the good-quality smokes!

That same evening shortly before prayers Pace and I sat by the fire where an oak log was smouldering among the brushwood. From time to time he blew cigarette-smoke rings towards the wood-smoke spiralling from the log. At last breaking the long silence, he whispered:

*"L'appartamento di Dom Mario è facile trovare."

Previously whenever I'd said I wanted to call on Dom Mario he had always changed the subject. Now obviously having overcome his misgivings, he continued:

*"Fa fronte alla stazione a Porto San Giorgio. Cerca la sua bicicletta appoggiata al muro. — Ma Arturo, va piano-piano! Ci sono molto tedeschi lì." Then, raising his voice, "Ecco Assunta e Caterina."

Little Caterina danced in ahead of the old lady who carried in her hand an empty bucket. The rest of the family followed close behind and, as soon as all were assembled, Pace began prayers . . .

The following afternoon I found the area fronting the station almost empty — just half-a-dozen Wehrmacht men lounging near the entrance. They took little interest in the shabby peasant parking his antiquated bicycle beside the priest's sturdy black roadster.

Dom Mario beamed at me as he led me up the stairs.

"Signor de Souza — or shall I say 'Arturo'? — I am very happy to see you again." He ushered me into his study which clearly also served as sitting-and-dining-rooms. The whole of one wall was lined with books. Near the window opposite was a small mahogany table and on the hob beside the log-fire facing me an iron kettle was singing. From a cupboard he produced a glazed earthenware tea-pot which he placed on a trevet to warm.

"Now I will surprise you. I make a real English cup of tea."

While he busied himself he continued talking:

"Marcelli Primo told me you had escaped — he is a good man, that one!" (as he laid the linen cloth).

* Dom Mario's flat is easy to find.
* It's opposite PORTO SAN GIORGIO railway station. Look for his bicycle leaning against the wall. But go very carefully. There are a lot of Germans about.

"Seventeen days under that weighbridge — incredibile!" (as he drew up the chairs).

"You were lucky the tedeschi soldiers didn't find you. They'd have shot you, of course!" (as he hitched up his soutane, stooping to make the tea).

"You know there's a price on your head," (as he reverently placed the tea-pot on the tea-pot stand).

"Eighteen hundred lire!" (as he slid a cosy over the pot).

"Very tempting to a poor man!" Then abruptly, "Hal Curtois wasn't on the camp newspaper, was he?" (as he set down a plateful of Genoese cakes).

I shook my head.

I took my place at the table, noting that his bookshelves were crammed with an assortment of popular fiction — Italian, French and English. Any theological works were presumably in his bedroom or at the seminary.

A train clanked to a halt. From where I sat I had a clear view of the station entrance and an oblique view of most of the platform. The six Wehrmacht men picked up their kit and strolled inside. Presently I caught sight of them entering a compartment In one of the front coaches.

Meanwhile I was telling the Dom all about Hal. At last I said what I had really come to say:

"Neither Hal nor I can thank you enough for passing our names to the Vatican radio. If it hadn't been for you our wives might never have known we were prisoners-of-war."

He spread his hands in deprecation, then invited:

"You will have a cake?"

I chose one before appreciatively sipping my tea.

"Now you must tell me about your home in England."

Whereupon I spoke of my love and of the Dorset lanes, of the Purbeck Hills, the quiet bays and the wide heath near Corfe where the Dartford Warbler sang. At last he stopped me, saying:

"Soon you will return to all that. Arturo, I pray for you."

I doubted whether he could in any practical way aid our escape, but the prayers of a true friend never come amiss . . .

As I left the house a column of trucks and armoured cars were roaring past the T-junction. It was all of ten minutes before I could cross the autostrada to take the little road back to Monte Urano.

In contrast to the military activity on the autostrada, life with the Brugnoni's at Monte Urano was a pastoral idyll: it was tempting just to go on enjoying their wonderful hospitality and hope that our troops would arrive some day to set us free.

"And meanwhile the family are in constant danger of being shot by the Germans and our own families are suffering unspeakable agony, having no news of us," commented Hal. We've got to make a move soon, Ken."

"Then we'll have to walk down to the Allied lines through the mountains. We'd never make it along the coast."

144

"Why not walk north and make for Switzerland?" suggested Hal.

"And be interned for the rest of the war?"

As Hal shook his head Caterina came skipping into the kitchen accompanied by Vincensina and Pierrino.

"Siamo pronto fare la scuola!" she announced as the three of them plumped themselves down at the table, preparing for lessons, text-books, exercise books and pencils at the ready . . .

With the turn of the month the weather deteriorated, periods of heavy rain alternating with cold days and frosty nights. We knew we would face terrible hardships in the mountains once winter really set in. Furthermore we were as sons of the family and it was clear the Brugnonis would do everything possible to persuade us not to leave.

"I'll tell them I'll go to see Giovanni when we get back to England," I said.

Giovanni, brother of Pace and Gino, had been a P.O.W. in Camp 63 somewhere in the U.K. for over a year. The family were extremely anxious, not having received a letter from him since early September.

Thus Hal and I were only waiting for an improvement in the weather. But in those first December days we had our alarms.

One morning as I was teaching the children and Hal was writing his diary: the fascisti did arrive. Their truck screeched to a halt in the cobbled yard, terrorising the poultry. There followed an unholy racket on the stairway as my boisterous pupils going down met the overwrought birds and bad-tempered fascisti coming up.

By the time peace was restored Hal and I had let ourselves down into the ox-stall by means of a trapdoor outside our bedroom, gone out from the front of the house and concealed ourselves in the finocchio-field.

We got to know the Tre-Tre and Marinello families quite well for in the evenings it was customary to go visiting, the neighbours' farmhouses each being about a quarter of an hour's walk. We would take a glass of wine, and, maybe a slice of home-made bread with homemade sausage. The families had their own wood-fired ovens and baked bread once weekly.

We also visited Vincensina's family. Mammina Giovanna closely resembled brothers Pace and Gino while Papa Guiseppe, heavily-moustached, smiled much but said little. Once he took us to his ox-stall to show us the marvel he had there perfected.

He pointed to a solid wooden wheel set vertically in a frame. A stick rather like a capstan-bar was loosely fitted into a hole a few centimetres in from the circumference.

He gripped the stick and, as he began to turn the wheel, a light bulb glowed above our heads. The faster the movement of the wheel, the brighter the bulb.

"E buono il dinamo?" asked Guiseppe triumphantly as the light shone brightly upon the champing oxen.

Hal who had traced the wires to and from the rotating magnetic core, nodded enthusiastically.

"Excellent! Really excellent!" he replied.

I was amused to think that Guiseppe's first concern had been for the animals: oil-lamps or candles were good enough for the humans.

Hal chided me:

"Don't you see, Ken? The animals are their livelihood!" . . .

On the afternoon of Wednesday, 1st December Dom Mario arrived at the farmstead. He cut a comical figure as, in his shovel-hat and long black robe he pedalled between the apple-trees, only dismounting when he reached the entrance. The poultry were strangely quiet in his presence, and he talked long and earnestly with Pace and Ines.

It was only as he was about to take his leave that he spoke to Hal and me. Standing at the kitchen door while a quorum of hens clucked inquisitively at the top of the steps, he gripped our arms and exhorted us:

"Buon' coraggio, Arturo! Buon' coraggio, Aroldo!"

Then he waved to the family, set the poultry scuttling away with a flap of his robe and hurried out of the house . . .

It may have been coincidence but the following Sunday, the family tried hard to persuade us to come to Mass up at Fermo, the shining white town on the nearby hill-top. We refused, loath to advertise our presence in the district.

I was surprised that the Brugnoni's should even have suggested our visiting Fermo where there was a strong presence of German soldiers. Maybe they had the idea that God called a truce on Sundays. Yet they should surely have known that, if he did, the Nazi soldiery would never observe it.

It was barely three weeks since Agostino had come running up the steps and burst into the kitchen crying, "They've taken Anselmo! They've taken Anselmo!"

The children were writing at the time, copying little texts that I had prepared. As Agostino flopped down on a bench, ten pencils clicked on the table and ten little frightened people stared open-mouthed at him.

Assunta was sieving at the madia and Ines was mixing the potato-flour for gnocchi. They stopped immediately and turned to the young man, terror in their faces.

"I visit the uncle of Carla at the mill in Fermo. I'd never seen so many tedeschi before. Nella piazza were many camione. Tedeschi behind me and in front of me as I walked. Subito the door opened and Marco grabbed my arm and pulled me into the mill."

" 'Quick!' he said, 'Prende quello sacco and carry it to the corner!' "

"As I lifted the sack of farina onto my shoulder, two tedeschi were looking in at the window. Then they walked on. There was shouting in the strada and the roar of camione. I looked out. They were prodding our men with guns, herding them into a big camione. And I saw the cousin of Carla,

146

Anselmo, there pleading with them, but they only laughed and took him away with the others."

Agostino had sobbed awhile, but neither Assunta nor Ines spoke, and the children sat still as statues.

"When the camione è andato gli altri tedeschi nella pizza walked away and there was no one, nessuno."

At last Ines had broken the silence: "Is bad, the war. Come Agostino, I make you a good cup of coffee."

Assunta with her back to us went on with the sieving while I noticed Caterina stoop to pick up her pencil.

"È rotta Arturo," she said.

I handed her a sharpened one before asking the Marinello boy, Umberto, "Che cosa hai scritto?"

Umberto stood up awkwardly, giving his ankle a painful knock on the leg of the table.

"Quando a Roma siamo condotti," he read hesitatingly, "Ognuno pensa per se e Dio per tutti."

"Arturo," asked Pierrino, "How do you say that in Inglese?"

Agostino was already drinking his coffee and the bambini were looking at me questioningly.

"When we are taken away to Rome, each one must take care of himself. But have no fear because God will protect us all."

As I translated I realised for the first time that, as I went about on the bicycle, I too ran the risk of being taken away for forced labour . . .

The following day there occurred an event which was to change all our escape plans.

A little before noon Gino and I were returning from the sheep-meadow along the avenue of lime-trees when a man appeared suddenly from behind the hurdle-fenced family latrine-ditch. As he ran to meet us Gino said:

"Si chiama Ettore. E communista. Non ha paura."

Ettore was agitated. Breathlessly he told Gino that he'd come to speak with me. Gino nodded and strolled on back to the house.

"Up there in Fermo," he panted, "Inglese paracudisti! — Tedeschi there too! — already one Inglese arrested! — your soldiers must leave the houses subito! — the people there very frightened!"

"Aspetti qui," I told him, "I will go and ask Pace if he can help."

As I expected Pace was in the stable rubbing down the old horse. He showed no surprise when I mentioned the tedeschi in Fermo: he'd seen them himself that very morning. However when I explained the predicament of the English soldiers he smiled at me reassuringly.

"Arturo, non si preoccupi! Certo, I will arrange all. The Tre-Tres and the Marinellos will help too. All is okay. You see!"

Thereupon he hurried away to meet Ettore while I went up to join the rest of the family at table.

147

CHAPTER 23

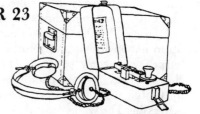

Buon' Natale

The soldiers came at dusk just as Hal and I were returning with armfuls of brushwood.

They were only three: Captain Cameron stocky, with weather-beaten face and dour expression, peaked cap mathematically straight; Lieutenant Darwall, tall, fresh-complexioned and broad-shouldered; and radio-operator, Corporal Brake, about Cameron's height, forage-cap rakishly perched on brown tufted hair, his sun-tanned features wrinkled in a permanent grin.

The fourth member of the unit, the Italian interpreter, his Calabrian dialect arousing suspicion, had been arrested. Also hors de combat was the radio slung around Brake's neck.

"The bloody battery's flat!" lamented the corporal.

"Leave it with me," offered Hal, "I'll fix it."

Brake looked at Captain Cameron who curtly nodded his permission. Then accompanied by Darwall carrying the battery, Hal and I went up to the bedroom, Gino taking Corporal Brake to the Tre-Tres and Pace conducting the Captain to the Marinellos.

We three slept that night and the following nights with Darwall the long dividing-line in the middle of the capacious bed, Hal and I curled up on either side.

Usually before sleeping Darwall would burble some nonsense about blowing up the autostrada bridge over the Tenna. It seemed that had been the original object of their enterprise when as Special Air Service they'd been landed by sea from a small boat.

We tried to explain that it would be pointless until the Allies began to advance. His reply was to point to his bag of fuses and explosives, saying:

"All good stuff, chaps! Pity not to use it!" . . .

Next morning, emptied vaso da notte in hand, I was crossing the yard on my way back from the latrine-ditch when I was amazed to see Darwall rush out of the ox-stall carrying a bucket. My first guess was that either he or Hal had been caught short and I blamed myself for being too previous in removing the pot. I was even more bewildered when Hal pursued Darwall brandishing what appeared to be a dagger. Momentarily I feared that the pair of them had taken leave of their senses and I approached warily, holding the vaso in front of me like a shield. Seeing my worried expression Hal grinned:

"It's all right Ken. We're going ice-collecting. Come and help us."

I saw then that the "dagger" was only a short blunt knife. As for the damnfool enterprise of ice-collecting, not for me to reason why, although on that bitter morning I didn't relish it.

However, by the time I'd thoroughly rinsed the vaso at the well, taken it up to our bedroom and returned downsteps through a flurry of hens, the bucket was nearly half-full. Darwall was tossing in wafers of ice as Hal chipped them from the puddles with the knife. Feigning enthusiasm, I joined in the fun working quickly despite numbed fingers until at last Hal said, addressing Darwall:

That'll do. Now in we go to boil it." Then turning to me he explained, "Distilled water you see Ken." . . .

By coffee-time two jugs of the precious liquid were cooling on the shelf near the sink.

Pace gulped down his coffee for it was market-day. We could hear the old black horse down below neighing impatiently.

We also drank hurriedly and were draining our mugs as Pace left the room.

*"Scusi! Anche noi andiamo fuori. Vogliamo aiutare Pace."

As it happened Pace did need our help and it wasn't until the laden cart was securely hitched that Hal was able to ask:

"Pace, do you think Giuseppe would let us use his dynamo to charge our battery?"

Pace said he knew his brother-in-law would be pleased to help. However he warned us to go carefully across the fields because there were places where we could be seen from the road.

Then, propping himself against the last of the finocchio-bundles, he cried "Olà!" to the horse and, to us, "Buona fortuna!"

We watched the cart until it was out of view beyond the orchard before returning upsteps to top up the battery with the distilled water.

We found Assunta alone in the kitchen, washing up crockery. She pretended not to notice what we were doing, but I saw that her lower lip was trembling.

As soon as we were ready we set off, Darwall joining me to help carry the heavy battery and Hal making for the Tre-Tre's to fetch Corporal Brake.

At first we were able to follow the footpath but later, to avoid being seen from the road, we had to negotiate a difficult detour. We slithered across ditches, scrambled through thorn-and-vine hedges, hoicked the battery over wire fences and finally arrived leg-weary and breathless.

Hal and Corporal Brake were already there, perched on boxes in the warmth of the stable sipping vino.

Giuseppe took the battery from us and wired it up to the dynamo. From his work-bench he selected a "capstan-bar" long enough to accommodate two turners.

* Excuse us. We're going out too. We'd like to help Pace.

150

CHAPTER 23   BUON' NATALE

Hal and Brake emptied their glasses, inserted the bar in the heavy wooden wheel and set to work immediately. It was our chance to sit and drink vino — but only for ten short minutes.

Darwall and I then endured ten long armcracking minutes.

At the end of two hours, Hal said he reckoned the battery should be sufficiently charged and, the carafe of wine being empty, we took our departure immediately . . .

We arrived back at the Brugnonis for our first ever meal of polentoni — huge maize-flour pancakes turned out directly onto the wooden table. They were dressed with small pieces of meat and tomato, and sprinkled with Parmesan cheese. There were twelve of us to share three polentoni. Each armed with a fork, Hal, Darwall, Brake and myself despatched ours without any border skirmishes . . .

Captain Cameron had ordered next day's briefing for two-fifteen, a quarter of an hour before listening-out period. While Corporal Brake set up the radio, Hal paid out the aerial through the bedroom window for me to carry the end of it up the ladder to the top of the haystack in the yard. Once I'd got my balance I thrust in Marinello's pitchfork vertically and looped the wire round the handle.

When I returned indoors Brake, earphoned and pencil at the ready, was tapping out our call-sign. After five minutes he shook his head and removed the phones.

"Can't raise 'em, Sir."

"Try them again Corporal. The buggers are probably playing cards!"

"More likely they've written us off after all this time!" interjected Darwall gloomily.

At that very moment the receiver started bleating Morse. Brake began writing, then stopped and put the headset down on the washstand.

"It's gone dead again, Sir. But Termoli wants us to be on air same time tomorrow."

Termoli was S.A.S. Headquarters.

Cameron clapped Hal on the shoulder.

"Thanks!" he said, "That's ten minutes transmission and reception — more than enough. Risky to be on the air too long anyway. Jerry'll D.F. us."

A whole morning's hard grind for ten minutes' juice! . . .

I was back at the Brugnonis in time for a short spell of reading, arithmetic and drawing before daylight began to fade.

At family prayers that night I prayed silently for my love. Maybe I'd be home for Christmas! . . .

Another exhausting morning at Giuseppe's charged the battery sufficiently for another ten minutes radio contact in the afternoon.

We waited breathlessly as Brake's pencil scratched rapidly in his notebook. Surely the S.A.S. would lay on a boat scheme to get us away.

At last Brake reported to Captain Cameron:

151

"H.Q. want info. about enemy reinforcements of men and material, specially what's going down by train."

It was a great disappointment. Of course we ought to have realised we were more valuable where we were. There was no point at all in getting us away.

"Acknowledge and switch off," Cameron instructed Brake. Then, "You chaps must realise we can't use Ettore for a job like this. He's first-class for message-carrying and contact with Italian families but I'm not trusting him with an Intelligence job. Darwall and I don't have the lingo nor should we go about openly in our uniforms unless it is absolutely necessary. Hal also must keep off the roads. — You're a typical Anglo-Saxon, Hal. They'd probably pick you up as a Jerry deserter!"

He paused, looking at me questioningly. They were all looking at me.

"O.K.," I said, "The Brugnoni's bike and I will do it."

There was not too much traffic on the autostrada that day — the occasional armoured car, the even-more-occasional staff car, and a few motorbikes and trucks.

Although Dom Mario received me as courteously as before, his usual wide smile was lacking, his expression pensive. Without uttering a word he made tea and emptied a few biscuits out of his tin.

A truck drew up down below and a couple of soldiers dismounted and entered the station. Then a motor-cycle crossed my line of vision — otherwise the area seemed completely deserted.

"There is much to see from the window?" enquired my host, pouring the tea.

"Just two German soldiers and a truck," I replied, embarrassed at being caught in the act.

He shook his balding pate sadly as he pushed across the plateful of biscuits.

"Sometimes I cannot hear myself speak for the noise of soldiers and their machines," he lamented "They find it convenient to pause here on their way from Ancona and the north. Maybe they have a Schnapps or a sausage before continuing down to the battlefront. The return traffic is not so heavy although one sees many ambulances."

He paused, fixing me with a penetrating stare.

"I suppose the station is also busy?" I asked casually.

"The Germans prefer the autostrada. Up to now they've used the railway very little." He added mischievously, "Why not keep watch while you have your tea? — Oh, please help yourself to another biscuit. — Look! A train is just coming in. Those two dismounting, they are fascisti from Civitanova and there are your two Germans boarding the next coach. They'll be returning from leave."

A smile flickered across his face and in that moment I knew that he knew!

After all, who would know the secrets of a parish better than its priest? Especially a priest who cared so deeply for his flock, who visited everybody,

152

who heard all their confessions, who spent longtime prattling happily with their children.

His next words proved that he was aware of the S.A.S. radio transmitter.

"You should tell your navy not to bombard our little farms, killing our animals, damaging our houses. Arturo, why do they do this?"

For a moment I was puzzled. Then I thought of the explosions Hal and I had become accustomed to hearing. We'd always ascribed them either to German target-practice or to the partigiani (if Italian partisans really did exist somewhere!)

"One good family had three oxen killed last week and the stable in ruins!"

"Yes?" I said.

"Do you think the country people will be friendly to the British if such atrocities continue?"

"No," I said.

"Tell them, Arturo! Please tell them!" he pleaded.

"If I can," I said.

Upon which he cheered up, poured me a second cup and produced some more Genoese cakes.

We remained train-watching for another twenty minutes before I took my leave . . .

The afternoon was already fading into evening when, pedals and chain creaking and mudguards rattling, I crossed the poultry-yard and put the bike back in the stable . . .

Three days later we charged the battery again and Brake sent through our report.

Again the response from Termoli was not quite what Hal and I expected but it was certainly more encouraging:

"We need twenty-two for the boat. Advise us when your party is ready."

"Acknowledge and switch off, and you two get the aerial down off the haystack as smart as you can."

While Hal and I scrambled about in the straw, through the window we could see Cameron and Darwall conferring.

They fell silent as we re-entered the bedroom and returned the rolled-up aerial to Brake.

"There's a job for each of you," Cameron told us. "Hal, it's your responsibility with Corporal Brake to ensure the battery's as fully-charged as possible. Next transmission we'll send the names of all the people in the escape party."

"How soon will that be?" asked Hal.

"That depends on Ken . . . Ken, the main task is to contact the major. He was at the mill but, if he's moved away, you'll have to track him down. He'll inform most of the others. There'll be a couple of other addresses you'll have to go to. Meanwhile I'll ask Ettore to fix up all the rendezvous."

One couldn't just march twenty-two would-be escapers through enemy-occupied country. They had to move in twos and threes to various houses, finally meeting at the forward rendezvous near the coast . . .

When we got back we found that the old sow had escaped into the orchard. Pace and Gino were flourishing sticks and swearing at her but in the mud she dodged them easily.

We joined in enthusiastically. At last Hal shouted, "Get back in, you fat slob!" Hal's English, being rude and to the point, did the trick. The sow turned and trotted back obediently.

Alas! just as Pace was about to secure the gate there was a sudden roar overhead. Looking up, we beheld a Spitfire diving straight for us! As it levelled out just above apple-tree height the terrified sow bolted, then fell on her side and slithered a good fifteen feet in the mud!

It took us till dusk to get her back!

"Probably a Spit, from P.R.U.," remarked Hal. However those Photographic Reconnaissance Unit boys usually flew high and straight and level.

Maybe the pilot of this one had been asked to say a special "How d'you do!" to us . . .

Next morning after a short session with the children, I set off for the mill. It was the same one we had passed the day Primo had brought us to the Brugnonis.

It wasn't until I'd turned at the crossroads that I became aware of an approaching car. I pedalled on steadily as it slowed down and stopped a little way ahead of me — a Mercedes, open-topped, the hood pushed back.

Two immaculate Wehrmacht officers were waving to me. I paused opposite them, one British-booted foot on the ground.

"Dov'è il cinema al Fermo?" demanded the oberleutnant in jerky incorrect Italian.

I waved my arm exactly as Pace or Gino would have done and called back in Ascoli dialect:

"Al dritta! Sempre al dritta!"

They looked in the direction of my wave, saw the shining little town on the hill-top, grinned, nodded and drove on.

I didn't even know if there was a cinema at Fermo. Perhaps it was an euphemism for the local brothel . . .

I waited until the Germans were out-of-sight before turning in at the mill.

At first the miller and his wife treated me with suspicion but when I mentioned the name "Cameron" all was well and I was ushered into the presence of the major. He told me that at the P.O.W. Camp at Modena they'd received no orders at all from Allied Command at the time of the Italian Armistice. He and some fellow-officers had simply walked out . . .

During Advent each of the contadini families slaughtered a pig, then made the whole thing into sausages and salami. We spent one evening at the Marinellos drinking their wine and helping make their sausages. The following evening we were at the Tre-Tres and the evening after that it was the Brugnoni's turn for sausage-making and receiving the neighbours.

The next task, akin to putting up paper-chains in England, was to hang the strings of sausages from one end of the kitchen to the other. The big salami were suspended vertically like long balloons! Smoke from the spacious fireplace would in time complete the manufacturing process.

If during a meal any of us received a tap on the shoulder it was either an alighting pigeon or a falling sausage! . . .

The battery stood up to the test when Corporal Brake sent the escape-party list for vetting at H.Q. Our departure date was then fixed for ten days before Christmas.

Captain Cameron briefed me to visit the various rendezvous to make sure they were still available and not, for instance, occupied by Germans as sometimes happened. The contadini also needed to know what time to expect us.

"The MTB will arrive at twentytwo-hundred hours so we have all to be at the forward rendezvous by twentyone-thirty. Remember if weather conditions are favourable the Navy boys could be early."

As it turned out weather conditions were anything but favourable. Black clouds were gathering when we three left the Brugnonis. The women were weeping for us, watching us depart, as they thought, to our certain death.

At our intermediate rendezvous we were told that the Germans had been there that very afternoon to take some poultry. The contadini were obviously very frightened and we were glad when the time came for us to go.

Captain Cameron gave his final briefing for the operation, all twenty-two of us gathered in the kitchen of the house overlooking the autostrada.

"We have fifteen minutes to wait before moving down to the beach. Because of this weather the boat may be delayed but it's up to us to be ready to rendezvous on time. If it blows up really badly they won't come at all. Darwall, Brake, the major and I will stay here. The rest of you will disperse around the farm."

As he spoke Lieutenant Darwall was at the window looking out across the barbed-wire-lined autostrada and over the railway embankment at the sea.

"There shouldn't be any patrols along the road for a couple of hours," added Cameron, "All the same be on your guard!"

Hal and I sat on straw in the stable in the company of an English school-teacher. Neatly-dressed and elegant, she contrasted absurdly with the mucky surroundings. In the adjoining stall a horse suffering from colic punctuated our conversation with rasping interjections.

And all the time the weather was deteriorating. Rain pattered, then drummed on our roof. When the drumming eased off, wild scuds slapped, one after another, against our sea-facing wall.

Fifteen minutes dragged by, thirty, forty-five and, by the time an hour was up, the wind was shrieking like a crazed banshee and rattling every timber in the place.

Presently Darwell appeared at the entrance, drenched, flapping his arms disconsolately.

"It's all off, chaps!" he shouted, "We're going back now!" The female "chap" got to her feet, bade us goodnight, and, fastening her rain-hat, walked out into the howling darkness. We never saw her again! . . .

Thereafter in dribs and drabs the other members of the party melted away, leaving the five of us marching back along the country lane like a drill squad, the three S.A.S. men in their khaki uniforms. In the canvas bag slung round his neck Hal carried the radio, Darwall had among other things his precious bridge-blowing equipment, Cameron his revolver, Brake the Schmeisser while I apprehensively clutched a hand-grenade.

Suddenly above the hum of the nearby mill we heard the sound of an approaching engine.

Comical as in a bedroom farce we tumbled into the ditch, Hal rolling face down into the mud as he cradled the radio.

A fraction of a second later we would have been seen and would have had to fight it out. As it was we lay there until the German truck had splashed by and was out of earshot. Maybe it was only making a routine visit to P.G.70 camp, maybe they were looking for us.

In either case, extreme caution was vital. Dirty, exhausted and soaked to the skin, we slunk back to the farms we had so recently left.

The Brugnonis were overjoyed to see us again. Hal, Darwall and I slept right through that day and the following night as well! . . .

CHAPTER 24

Naked to Freedom

So it was Christmas at the Brugnonis under a festoon of sausages, feasting upon chicken and veal, finishing up the sausages left over from the previous manufacture and all with copious helpings of homegrown vegetables, finocchio predominating.

Gino now presented Caterina with the family of exquisitely-carved wooden dolls he had been creating during the preceding months. Stella and Ines had made doll's-clothes and Caterina was delighted and immediately absorbed.

We afterwards discovered that Gino's sculpted animals were *Babbo Natale's present for Vincensina; the soldiers for Pierrino.

The family tried so hard to persuade me to go to Mass, but I preferred to listen to Caterina who, having dressed the dolls and sat them on the window-sill, got me out of a difficult situation by pleading:

†"Arturo, vieni giocare colle pecore!"

I lifted the little girl onto my shoulders and we made our way down the stradicella between the limetrees to the meadow where the sheep were grazing.

When I set her down she ran and put her arms round the neck of a black-and-white lamb. On Christmas morning no gesture could have been more appropriate . . .

The first fortnight of January, 1944 was taken up in locating our escape party and preparing for a second attempt. We sought replacements for the two or three we couldn't find.

I had one encounter with a couple of genuine fascists whom I feared more than the Germans. Although I looked and sounded like a local contadino, my vocabulary was limited and I dared not get into long conversation.

This time the topography saved me. I was coming down from Fermo and met them near the crest of a hill.

"Ciao!" I greeted with a cheery wave and a hearty thrust of the pedals.

"Ciao!" I heard their reply above the wind as I free-wheeled down the steep gradient.

They were not local men, possibly the couple from Civitanova. Nearly all the Ascoli fascisti were fascisti in name only. To obtain any worthwhile job one had to represent oneself as a fascist.

* Father Christmas
† Let's go and play with the sheep!

157

ESCAPE FROM ASCOLI

The night of the 21st January was starlit with only the merest trace of cloud. This time the forward rendezvous was a house farther down the coast. Cameron showed me the map pointing to the grid-reference position we had to reach by 22.30 hours.

"About 200 yards north of the river-mouth," he said, "You're a navigator, Ken. Will you please lead us?"

I put my own finger on the position of the farm and nodded.

It looked easy. Bearing 100 degrees, three quarters of a mile.

But, glancing out of the window, I wondered how easy that three quarters of a mile would be. The moon had risen, not full but bright and revealing. I shuddered at the prospect of crossing the skyline of the railway embankment!

Cameron read my thoughts.

"We've timed it to miss the autostrada patrols," he assured me.

We made our way down the stone steps which, unlike the Brugnoni's, were outside the building. At the bottom Darwall thrust the torch into my hand.

"You'll need this, Ken," he whispered.

Seeing my obvious bewilderment he added:

"Of course you won't shine it unless absolutely necessary. But you'll want it for signalling."

"Signalling?" I repeated.

"Don't you remember Termoli's instructions? We have to identify ourselves to the boat at 22.30 hours. Send R-repeat-R."

I remembered all right, but when Brake had read out the radio message I little thought I'd be the Aunt Sally standing at the water's edge with the torch.

"Suppose it isn't our boat. Suppose it's a German E-boat."

Cameron had said E-boats did sometimes use the river mouth. The last of our party, a burly South African, had by now descended the steps.

Chuckling hugely at what he construed as my hilarious sense of humour, Darwall gave me a gorilla-like clap on the back and we set off across a meadow, the faithful Pole Star dead in line with my left shoulder. A 90-degree course to the autostrada and railway embankment was shortest and therefore safest. After that we could make a southerly alteration.

We reached the barbed wire without incident, Darwall having the wire-cutters at the ready. I was fascinated by the sure way he breached the intricate convolutions, only cutting exactly where necessary.

In a matter of seconds his gloved hands were holding back the strands for us. We all huddled up together waiting for the signal.

"Now!" whispered Cameron.

We scrambled across as soundlessly as we could all except the burly South African who blundered into a pile of empty tin-cans which someone had carefully stacked by the roadside.

Darwall released the wire and raced across to us.

"Get down all of you — flat and don't move!"

CHAPTER 24   NAKED TO FREEDOM

Move! We hardly dared breathe!

We just lay there on the ground beside the road petrified as the tins clattered and went on clattering.

A dog began barking in a nearby farmyard on the coastal side of the road. Other dogs joined in. A window was slammed open and a man began swearing at the dogs. At intervals more tins rolled down, striking high or low notes according to their size. Then a woman began screeching at the man.

Such a hullaballoo can never before have devastated the peace of an Adriatic night!

I expected every moment the arrival of the enemy, sure that the whole enterprise was about to end in a murderous shoot-out.

Incredibly nothing happened! The last mobile tin stopped rolling, the dogs stopped howling, the couple stopped shouting and the window finally closed.

Darwall gave me what was intended as a gentle nudge and jerked his head in the manner of a man inviting his companion into a pub.

We hadn't gone more than fifty paces before, all of a sudden, my anxiety changed to relief. We were heading straight for a culvert! No need to climb over the embankment.

When we stooped to walk through it Hal murmured, "Well done, Ken!" However I couldn't take the credit. Doubtless the culvert had been spotted on the photos taken back by the Spitfire.

A further hundred paces, branching south-east, brought us to an empty trench into which we all thankfully tumbled.

By Hal's watch, the time was twenty minutes past ten. As we strained eyes and ears for signs of the boat a divine hand drew a curtain of cloud across the moon.

After the longest five minutes of my life, above the quiet lap of the sea we heard the faint throbbing of an engine. I climbed out onto the beach, going down to the water's edge, peering into the grey distance.

The throbbing grew louder. A tiny patch of that grey darkened and took substance. The throbbing stopped. I aimed the torch.

"Short-long-short," I flashed. Then repeated more slowly, "R repeat R . — . . — ."

Two responses were possible. A hail of bullets if it were an E-boat. If not, the approach of our rescuers.

A thin moonbeam, penetrating a tear in the cloud-curtain, lit up a yellow patch in the water — a rubber dinghy!

Soon I could see it was one of a pair being towed by a rowing-boat. The muffled oars rose and fell, rose and fell, were then held horizontal, motionless as the bows scrunched gently on the beach.

My companions were all around me now, wading out to the dinghies. I followed the S.A.S men, Hal and one or two others into the rowing-boat, falling rather than sitting as one of the crew shoved us off.

Cameron and Darwall each took a spare oar.

159

ESCAPE FROM ASCOLI

"Ken," said Cameron, "would you hold my boots, please?"

I slipped the torch back into Darwall's satchel and, without asking the reason why, took the heavy boots into my care.

Four men strained at the oars of the overloaded boat. We were low in the water at the outset but the effort of towing caused the stern to dip lower and lower at every thrust.

The water splashed over us and swilled about our ankles. Nor was it possible to make a move to bale out. Any further movement would have caused the boat to sink forthwith.

Somehow it stayed afloat even when the water was up to our waists! Twenty or thirty yards from what we now recognised as a motor torpedo-boat, abruptly, it sank. I was left treading water and holding Cameron's boots high above my head. It may have been some satisfaction to him to know that they were the last items to get wet.

I dropped them into the icy water, kicked off my own boots and breast-stroked through the bit of the Adriatic that lay between me and the Royal Navy.

Only when they hauled me aboard did I discover they weren't the Royal Navy but the Reggia Marina. Anyway they were on our side now so it didn't matter.

Together with a number of other sodden, dripping men I took refuge in the warmth of the engine-room. In a few seconds our clothes were disposed on pipes or hooks, and a pride of goose-pimpled naked men were warming themselves by running frantically on the spot.

At that the boat began to move — cross between a mobile Greek gymnasium and a Chinese laundry. And how it moved! A speed of around 45 knots brought us to Termoli within five hours and without incident.

Dressed in damp-warm clothes I stepped off the gangplank on to Allied territory.

"Come on in fellers and have a cupper char," an S.A.S. officer greeted us.

Huge mugs of tea laced with rum — we raised them in silent toast to Freedom. But the only word we uttered was "Thanks!"

Our evasion had been a drama in three acts: desert trek, curtain descending on the enemy camp, escape from the prison-camp which left us in enemy-occupied territory, and now this unforgettable cupper char signalling the final curtain of the final act of evasion.

CHAPTER 25

Home

As HMT Ranchi docked at Greenock the band was playing on the quayside. We disembarked expecting a hero's welcome and were only prevented from kissing the rain-washed paving by the arrival of a Military Police jeep.

"Ye're to accompany us to the station!" commanded the grim-faced Scottish sergeant, lightly touching his revolver-holster. We scrambled into the back of the jeep to be whisked away to Glasgow Central railway station. There under escort we were ushered into a train, locked in a Third-Class compartment and told we'd be let out when we reached our destination. Fortunately the compartment had an adjoining lavatory. Nevertheless we both felt we'd already had enough of being locked in railway trains . . .

In contrast the English M.P. who unlocked the door at King's Cross was smiling and friendly.

"Follow me, fellers," he grinned, "We've got a cab waiting for you."

And there it was — a real London taxi! We sank back on the soft leather upholstery to watch dear old battle-scarred London glide by — Marble Arch, Oxford Street, Piccadilly and the rest, finally arriving at Adastral House for R.A.F. Interrogation.

We gave exactly the same answers to exactly the same questions we'd been asked at Army Interrogation at Termoli. But this time we had a question of our own, the one which had been haunting us for fifteen long months:

"Any news of the rest of our crew, Sir?" It was Hal who finally blurted it out.

The Interrogating Officer put down his tea-cup to refer to the papers in front of him.

"Sergeants Coles, Prosser and Bullock are now prisoners-of-war in Germany," he informed us. Then looking up and smiling, he added, "Sergeant Frampton made it back to Base after eleven days. He walked south to Siwa Oasis." He paused to study the effect of this announcement.

"Good for Alf!" I exclaimed, "However did he manage it?"

"Like you fellows he had a large slice of luck. First day he found the crashed aircraft and topped up with water. Next he met up with a 70-Squadron Wellington crew. Sadly three of them dropped with exhaustion, but Sergeant Frampton and the survivors were befriended by an Arab family who escorted them to Siwa. There, they were picked up by a British staff car from Advanced Air Headquarters."

161

"Where is he now, Sir?" asked Hal.

"I've jotted down the number of his squadron and other details for you. Maybe you two Londoners will be able to get together sometime?" So saying he ripped a sheet from his memo-pad and passed it to Hal. Then abruptly curtailing the interview "Now you chaps better get away. Got your passes?"

He shook hands with us before we went . . .

Once out in the street we knew that it was all over and that we were free, free to do what we'd been planning to do for so many months — go home to our wives! Three weeks leave stretched before us like the promise of Heaven . . .

Waiting in the aircraft factory office I could hear the radio being played through loudspeakers outside. Our own favourite, Ann Shelton, was singing.

Then my love came in, still in cap and factory overall, and for one precious moment the world stood still. Everything around us ceased to exist . . .

The sun was just breaking through as, arm-in-arm, we set off for home. The words of the song reached us through the open workshop window. It was the German soldiers' song I'd heard a life-time ago at Derna.

"I knew you were waiting there for me
You'd always be
My own Lilli Marlene."

Neat barrack-huts set in a broad meadow, barbed-wire inconspicuous, the brown-clad POWs well-fed and well-cared-for — this was the camp to which the Kirkcaldy bus had brought me, fresh from calling on Andy Arnot's folks in Links Street.

"We was expecting you," grinned a Pioneer-Corps sergeant as, my War-Office pass in his hand, he conducted me across to the huts.

I recognised Giovanni immediately, both from the photos the Brugnoni's had shown me and because of his strong resemblance to Pace and Gino. However he was fairer than his brothers, sported a pencil moustache, his features more delicate, his expression studious.

That afternoon we walked the country lanes beside fields dotted with little round haystacks exactly like the one at the Tre-Tre's which had, in days long-gone, served to support an aerial.

I reassured him about his family, telling him about the German cigarettes I got for Pace; about Assunta making soap and Gino making toys; about little Caterina and the lambs; about all the incidents I could remember in the lives of his family during the three months they had cared for me as their son.

Giovanni knew his own homecoming was not far away. Therefore he was happy to hear how, after long aching separation, I had come home once more to Lillian, my own love . . .

ABOUT THE AUTHOR

Warrant Officer Ken de Souza shortly
after his escape and return to England

Born at Langley Marsh, Buckinghamshire, Ken de Souza was educated at Highgate School where he became involved in starting and editing magazines and setting up a printing press in the loft of one of the School Houses. Leaving school he contributed stories of rural life to "The Wiltshire News" and won a poetry prize in a national Sunday newspaper. He was selected to represent Wiltshire against Gloucestershire in a benefit cricket match for Walter Hammond, the future England captain.

From Steeple Ashton, Wiltshire the family moved to Bournemouth where Ken met Lillian the girl across the road. They married four years later and have recently celebrated their Golden Wedding. They have two children and two grown-up grandchildren.

Prior to the outbreak of war, in between playing cricket for Bournemouth Sports Club Ken worked for an insurance company. In May 1940 he joined the R.A.F. as Air Observer, and in June, 1942 he and his crew began operations with 148 Squadron Wellingtons (Middle East) . . .

After his escape and return to the U.K. he spent five pleasant months in the Lake District as Air Navigation instructor, then a period with Transport Command, 511 Squadron flying Yorks, and was one of the crew nominated for the inaugural flight to Ceylon (Sri Lanka).

On demob, he returned briefly to insurance, now earning much more than the meagre pre-war crust. However all Ken wanted was to continue the career he had already started haphazardly — in a small way back in Italy with the bambini — the career of teaching. He was accepted for Cooper's Hill, an L.C.C. Teacher Training College. After qualifying he taught in Poole Junior and Middle Schools until 1982 in various posts. He organised the pairing of Poole school-children with Parisian school-children culminating in the first-ever exchange visits undertaken by a Junior school in Poole.

After gaining the M.C.C. Youth Coaching Certificate with Hants C.C.C. he forsook his own game to concentrate on bringing along young cricketers-

163

to-be. He and his pupils also contributed to the P.E. teaching film, "Free to Move".

Since retirement he has at least set down just as he remembers it, the story of his wartime escape.

KendeSouza.

ROYAL AIR FORCES ESCAPING SOCIETY

(Registered under the War Charities Act 1940)
R.A.F.E.S. CHARITABLE FUND
(Registered under the Charities Act 1960)

SIR LEWIS HODGES
ALLENS HOUSE
PLAXTOL
SEVENOAKS
TN15 0QZ
KENT (0732) 810255

President
AIR CHIEF MARSHAL Sir LEWIS M. HODGES
K.C.B., C.B.E., D.S.O., D.F.C.
Chairman:
CAPTAIN F. H. DELL.
Secretary:
Mrs. E. LUCAS HARRISON

206 BROMPTON ROAD
LONDON SW3 2BQ
01-584 5378

ROYAL AIR FORCES ESCAPING SOCIETY (reg. under the War Charities Assn.)

The RAF Escaping Society is unique amongst charities with the aim of maintaining contact with thousands of patriots who helped members of the RAF to evade capture and so return to their units.

It was formed in 1945 as an immediate reaction from the thousands of successful evaders and escapers who wanted their Helpers rewarded for their bravery and their help, given at a staggering cost. The penalties if caught aiding airmen were severe, usually execution by firing squad or imprisonment in a concentration camp, where thousands died. The number of Helpers was vast. No-one knows exactly how many lost their lives, but they achieved wonderful results. In Europe alone 2,803 British and Commonwealth airmen were brought back. In 1945 more than 14,000 Helpers were alive to be recognised officially as having given significant assistance to the Royal Air Force.

The Society was founded by Marshal of the Royal Air Force Viscount Portal of Hungerford, then Chief of Staff, who became its first President. The first Chairman — from 1946 to 1957 — was Air Chief Marshal Sir Basil Embry, himself an escaper.

The main strength of the Society is in its nucleus in the United Kingdom, with strong support from active contigents in Australia and Canada. Only successful evaders and escapers are eligible for membership, a rule which has the disadvantage of a steadily diminishing membership.

Through its many contacts with its Helpers the Society achieves much in promoting friendship and goodwill, which explains why it is far better known on the Continent than in Britain.

Whenever a Helper is found to be in need the Society responds at once with practical and, usually, financial assistance. This work has been carried on from its inception.

The next five years are critical. The Society has to raise every penny to function. There is no despondency: as the task becomes more demanding so the challenge is accepted as the more exciting. The Society will maintain its aim and stay in being until the reason for its formation has gone. This steadfast intention was expressed when Lord Portal decided that our motto should be: "LET US ALWAYS REMEMBER THOSE WHO HELPED US WHEN WE WERE IN NEED."

YOU can help the Society in many ways: you can make a donation or enter into a four-year Covenant. BETTER STILL, FOR A MINIMUM SUBSCRIPTION OF £4 p.a. YOU CAN BECOME "A FRIEND OF THE SOCIETY" and, at our annual Party, meet many of those fascinating people from abroad who are the reason for our continued existence.

ROYAL AIR FORCES ESCAPING SOCIETY

**206 BROMPTON ROAD
LONDON SW3 2BQ
01-584 5378**

MEMBERSHIP CARD

Name .... K. de Souza ....

Year ... 1984 ...

No 800 .... E. Surgo Hamish ... Secretary

- -

* Please register me as a FRIEND OF THE RAF ESCAPING SOCIETY and send my Membership Card together with your Newsletter. I enclose s.a.e. and cheque for £_____

* Please send me a Bankers Order/Covenant Form. Upon completion and return I will receive my Membership Card and your Newsletter.

* My donation of £_____ to your Charitable Fund and s.a.e. for acknowledgement are enclosed.

* Please delete paragraphs not applicable.

NAME _____

ADDRESS _____

_____ POST CODE _____

To: The Secretary, RAF Escaping Society, 206 Brompton Road, London. SW3 2BQ
Tel: 01 584 5378